WAR
on TWO
FRONTS

WILLIAM BOOTH'S
THEOLOGY *of* REDEMPTION

CREST
BOOKS

Copyright © 2017 by The Salvation Army

Published by Crest Books

Crest Books
The Salvation Army National Headquarters
615 Slaters Lane
Alexandria, VA 22313
Phone: 703/684-5523

Lt. Col. Allen Satterlee, Editor-in-Chief and National Literary Secretary
Roger Selvage, Art Director
Nick Holder, Editorial Assistant

Available in print from crestbooks.com and in ebook form from wphstore.com

ISBN: 978-0-9913439-9-7

Printed in the United States

DEDICATION

This book is dedicated with love to my wife Karen. It is beyond all doubt that without her love, support, and encouragement throughout a long and sometimes tedious PhD program, I would never have completed the program and been granted the degree. Without such support this study would not have been written, and this book would not have been a possibility. These accomplishments are hers as well as mine.

Thank you, Karen.

TABLE OF CONTENTS

ABOUT THE AUTHOR

Roger J. Green is the son of Salvation Army officers, born in Boston, Massachusetts in 1943. He recently retired as Professor of Biblical and Theological Studies at Gordon College in Wenham, Massachusetts where he also held the Terrelle B. Crum Chair of Humanities. He taught for three years at Asbury College, and taught for forty-three years at Gordon College. He served for twenty-six years as the department chair. He led Gordon College's Holy Land Pilgrimage every other year. In 2015 he was awarded with the Lifetime Achievement Award, and a scholarship was named for him as the Roger J. Green/Salvation Army Scholarship.

Dr. Green received his B.A. from Temple University in Philadelphia; his M.Div. from Asbury Theological Seminary; his M.Th. from Princeton Theological Seminary; and his Ph.D. from Boston College. He was awarded the D.D. (honorary) from William and Catherine Booth College (now Booth University College).

He has held memberships in the American Academy of Religion, the American Society of Church History, the Evangelical Theological Society, the International Bonhoeffer Society, the Karl Barth Society of North America, and the Wesleyan Theological Society. He serves on the Board of Directors and the Steering Committee of the Wesleyan Holiness Connection, the Academic Oversight Advisory Council for The Salvation Army College for Officer Training in the USA Eastern Territory, the Board of Advisors for the Institute for Congregational Trauma and Growth, and the Board of Advisors for The Salvation Army Center for Holiness Studies. He is a Vice President of The Salvation Army Historical &

Philatelic Association in London, England, and is a research fellow for the Australasian Centre for Wesleyan Research.

He has written articles in several journals, and was a contributor to *The Wesley Study Bible*, *The Reflecting God Study Bible*, and *Invitation to the Classics*. However, much of his scholarship has been devoted to the history and theology of The Salvation Army. His books include *War on Two Fronts: The Redemptive Theology of William Booth* (The Salvation Army); *Catherine Booth: a Biography of the Co-Founder of The Salvation Army* (Baker Books); *The Life and Ministry of William Booth, Founder of The Salvation Army* (Abingdon Press); and *Boundless Salvation: The Shorter Writings of William Booth* (Peter Lang Publishers), which he co-edited with Andrew Eason. His books have been translated into Spanish, German, Chinese and Korean. He is a co-editor of *Word & Deed: A Journal of Salvation Army Theology and Ministry*, which is now in its nineteenth year. His thirty-year proposal for an International College for Soldiers finally was inaugurated by The Salvation Army in September of 2012.

Dr. Green was a member of the Army's International Spiritual Life Commission, and was the first soldier appointed to the Army's International Doctrine Council. In 2012 he was admitted to the Order of the Founder. He travels internationally for The Salvation Army, preaching and lecturing at officers' councils, soldiers' retreats, and Brengle Institutes, and attending conferences. He ministers throughout the United States and Canada, and in addition has ministered in Argentina, Australia, Brazil, Chile, England, Finland, Hong Kong, Korea, New Zealand, Nigeria, Scotland, South Africa, Sweden, Taiwan, Wales, and Zambia, in some territories ministering several times.

He and his wife, Karen, live in Danvers, Massachusetts and attend the corps in Old Orchard Beach, Maine.

PREFACE

What you will read in the following pages is the beginning, not the end. This book is the outgrowth of what was originally a dissertation, written in fulfillment of the requirements for a PhD from Boston College. Such is written on a topic not yet researched in the scholarly world. It is also written under the watchful eye of an advisor and a committee, and must conform to the demands as well as to the idiosyncrasies of such people. Not written originally for the general public, this work was prepared under many restrictions which are not the case when one is writing for sheer pleasure alone. The first edition was published by the USA Southern Territory of The Salvation Army.

Given the many strictures of such a work, there was some hesitation in making even part of it available in book form. However, I present this to the serious reader, and especially to my fellow Salvationists, in the hope that it will cause reflection upon our common theological heritage and stimulate us to more extensive and careful consideration of that theology. I envision this work not as some final and definitive statement of the theology of William Booth, but as an initial inquiry into such theology. My own research on this topic still continues to this day, and others will certainly follow with greater clarity, better insight, and keener skills for continued research into our theological history. Much work yet remains to be done not only in this area, but in the theology of other Army notables such as Catherine Booth, Bramwell Booth and George Scott Railton.

In this book are included many of the notes that were in the original dissertation. These may be helpful to those who are interested in further study of this material. Books and articles mentioned in the notes provide invaluable resources for such study.

This book is personal, written primarily as a result of my private study. This is not an official statement by The Salvation Army, and I affirm what was written by St. John Ervine in his preface to *God's Soldier: General William Booth*, that "no one but myself is responsible" for the contents of this book. Where there is insight into truth within the book, I gladly accept the credit. Likewise, I accept the blame for any errors in this work. The fault for such errors lies in me alone, and any critical challenge of the contents of the book must be directed at me personally and not at The Salvation Army.

My one regret with the first edition of this work is that I was not involved in the proofreading of the text. There were several unfortunate errors with the text, which have now been corrected. I can only pray that this second edition makes for an easier and more comprehensible reading of the text without concern for any errors. I have decided not to add much text to the original work. This book could easily expand to three volumes because so much research has been done since it was first published over twenty-five years ago. I have added to the text and mentioned some resources published after 1989 only where such additions are critically necessary and will be helpful to the reader.

Naturally, there are many people to whom I am indebted and would like to thank personally. Unfortunately, space does not permit such personal indulgence, but there are four people who must be given credit publicly. The first, my wife Karen, I have already thanked in the dedication, but my gratitude to her is boundless. Second, this book would never have been a possibility without the continued encouragement of Commissioner John D. Waldron. It was in many ways his kind but firm persistence that finally enabled this project to be completed. I was privileged to count him as a friend in so many ways and to share with him a love for all things Army, especially our history, tradition, and theology. And thirdly, I want to thank the Southern Literary Council, Mr. Ralph I. Miller, secretary, and Lt. Colonel Houston Ellis. Colonel Ellis was, at the time of the writing of the first edition, still very active in a ministry for which he is obviously gifted, and his assistance in this project made this all finally possible. And since the publication of the first edition I have heard from Salvationists around the world who have found this work helpful. I am ever grateful for that. However, I am quick to add that this second edition would not have been possible without the assistance and encouragement of National Literary Secretary and *War Cry* Editor-in-Chief Lt. Colonel Allen Satterlee. He and the members of his staff have been invaluable in giving life to this second edition.

It is my sincere hope that *War on Two Fronts: The Redemptive Theology of William Booth* will aid in a clearer understanding both of our theological heritage and thereby of ourselves. Should this be the case, perhaps the Army will be enhanced, and whenever that happens by the grace of God, the ultimate benefit belongs to the Kingdom of God in Christ.

Roger J. Green
Danvers, Massachusetts
August, 2015

INTRODUCTION

The Victorian England of William Booth

England in the Nineteenth Century

Victorian England was a country at peace, facing no serious threat to national security from outside forces or governments. However, the Industrial Revolution, beginning in the eighteenth century with the use of mechanical power for agricultural production and mass production in mining and manufacturing, was in full force by the time Queen Victoria came to the throne in 1837. That revolution was "not an event but a process."[1]

The growing cities became centers for the factory system that characterized the Industrial Revolution, and these cities were increasingly inhabited by men and women from the English countryside and from outside the island. Initially, two societies formed in Victorian England: the village society, characterized by farming and governed still by wealthy landowners to whom most people paid respect, and the increasingly urban society, characterized by manufacturing and governed democratically.

In spite of the distinction between village life and urban life initially brought about by the Industrial Revolution, eventually the two amalgamated: country life was absorbed into city life by an increasingly effective railway and transportation system and by the expansion of cities into the villages. Suburban life was born, and with it came the problems associated with the rise of England's urban centers. "With locomotion constantly diminishing the distance between the villages and the city, with the spread of science and machinery even in the process of agriculture, in a small island with a dense urban population that had now lost all tradition of country life, it was only a question of time before urban ways of thought and action would penetrate and absorb the old rural world, obliterating its distinctive features and local variations."[2] The tranquility of village life eventually dissolved, and the streets became mean as the Victorian period of English life evolved. Writing about East London, an area with which William Booth and his followers would become heavily involved, Sir Walter Besant noted that there was "no other city in the world in the least like East London for the unparalleled magnitude of its meanness and its monotony."[3]

For all the advantages brought about by the Industrial Revolution, it produced a kind of rampant individualism. Individuals were inspired by the thoughts of getting rich, and this often manifested itself in an attitude of self-help and a drive to make money. The strong embraced such individualism. The weak were often devastated and abused by it. The weak shared neither the wealth nor the power. With such individualistic drive for riches came a decrease in the quality of workmanship and craftsmanship.

As more people entered the competitive marketplace, new classes were created. The division between the few rich and the many poor began to break down, and various levels of middle classes and working classes arose. There was no financial competition for the extremely wealthy, but their standard of living was far above that of the unskilled laborers, the unemployed, and the unemployable who inhabited the slums of England.

A lack of planning plagued Victorian England. Not only was there a lack of social planning—various groups emerged as social and economic forces determined the direction of the Industrial Revolution—there was also a lack of urban planning of the Victorian cities, which grew rapidly and chaotically. East London, wrote one author, "is not a city by organization; it is a collection of overgrown villages lying side by side."[4] Trevelyan summarized such chaos in this way: "Man had acquired formidable tools for refashioning his life before he had given the least thought to the question of what sort of life it would be well for him to fashion."[5]

By 1851, half of England's population inhabited crowded, infested, chaotic English cities, and a decrease in the death rate meant an increase in population. A growing immigration population heightened the problem, and the cities could not cope with the rising tide. Chadwick's criticism is important here:

> The parish churches, the dissenting chapels, the Roman Catholic chapels, were not equipped to cope with this tide of immigrants. The churches and chapels were not unique. Nothing in the city was equipped to cope. Municipal government, building, sanitation, health, cemeteries, hospitals, roads, paving, lighting, police, dentists, schools—all the organs of city life were strained till they were bursting.[6]

The Industrial Revolution and the urban life that it had spawned had produced a crisis in Victorian England. The urban masses lived in extreme poverty, worked long hours in unsafe conditions, and vices both great and small crept into their lives. "The relative misery of the poor at this period as compared to that of their forebears is hard to estimate, for want of facts about earlier times. The absolute misery of many of them is a fact incontestable."[7]

Prostitution—exacerbated by the white slave trade, a low age of consent for girls, and economic instability for women—became a dominant part of urban life. Alcoholism pervaded society, and cheap literature made available to the masses further debased an already intolerable situation. Added to this was the burden upon the cities of the unemployed, the indigent, the sick, the hungry, and the homeless. And by the early 1870s there was a serious agricultural depression throughout England, caused by both crop failure at home and an increase in American grain imports.

However, all was not lost. The nineteenth century witnessed an increased exposure to the general public of the problems brought about by the Industrial Revolution. That came from two sources. First, there was a rising humanitarianism throughout the nineteenth century in England, often expressed through radical politics. This resulted in a systematic defense of the cause of the poor and the disenfranchised. Some of that humanitarianism was religiously based and some was not.

A second source was Evangelical religion which, whether manifested in the Anglican Church or in dissenting groups, nevertheless fostered a humanitarianism and provided" the moral cement of English society."[8] Evangelical religion and radical politics found themselves engaged in very similar endeavors, and as the nineteenth century progressed, the poverty of the masses and contingent problems increasingly came to public attention.

There were many avenues toward social reform. Colonization and emigration to the less-populated countries of Canada, Australia, and New Zealand did relieve some of the pressure of city life and slum existence in Victorian England. However, the combination of humanitarianism and Evangelical religious sympathies produced significant social reform in Great Britain itself, beginning with the abolition of the slave trade in England in 1807 and in the British Empire in 1833.

The dire plight of the working poor diminished with such legislation as the Trade Unions Act of 1825; the Factory Act of 1833, which put into place government inspectors to enforce its various requirements; the Mines Act of 1842; and the Ten Hours Bill of 1847. The welfare of the general public, particularly the poor, was served with such legislation as the Public Health Act of 1848, the Lunatic Asylums Act of 1853, and the Education Act of 1870. Such formal legislation was stimulated by a brand of journalism with a social conscience, represented by people like W. T. Stead and by both church and humanitarian organizations designed and determined to meet the needs of the poor with or without political endorsement. Pressure continued throughout the century for the public education of the poor, shorter working hours, safer working conditions, equitable wages, the emancipation of women, the enfranchisement of women largely through the efforts of Florence Nightingale and John Stuart Mill, and the establishment of law and order in the streets of the cities.

Contemporary literature of that age is filled with articles calling for such measures, and the pressure of opinion—Evangelical, humanitarian, public, and political—brought about measures for the improvement of conditions for the working classes, industrial training of destitute children, and open and competitive examination for the Civil Service. The emancipation of women received special attention during Victoria's reign, and these issues became crucial: the enfranchisement of women, the education of women, housing for women, and the entry of women into previously male-dominated professions such as medicine, journalism, and teaching. The issue of women in ministry would become important to William Booth, largely through the influence of his wife, Catherine Booth. The Victorian conscience even called for the more humane treatment of animals. It is fair to say that Victorians became indignant at certain evils. Reasonable and religious appeals to peoples' sense of right and justice had worked.

There is evidence that considerable improvements came by the end of Victoria's reign. Acknowledging that there was still much work to be done and much to be desired, Sir Walter Besant stated in *London in the Nineteenth Century* that "the great difference between the slum of 1798 and that of 1898 is the diminution of lawlessness."[9] The poor also benefited from the establishment of amusements, public museums and libraries, parks, an efficient postal system, treatment of alcoholism, the availability of inexpensive housing, and public baths and washhouses.

As has been mentioned often, there was a strong religious side to nineteenth-century England. Victorian England was religious, Chadwick reminds us.[10] There was a breadth of Christian traditions which existed side by side in a generally tolerant atmosphere. Society became less interested in religious questions as the Victorian age progressed, and Christians from many traditions drew closer together in seek of mutual support and encouragement. Political parties increasingly displayed class affiliation rather than religious loyalty. Social questions in the political arena were increasingly addressed by humanitarian sensitivities alone, apart from religious loyalties.

In spite of occasional "anti-papal" attitudes among Protestants, the Roman Catholic Church strengthened in England throughout the nineteenth century. This was due primarily to Irish immigration, the full force of which came as a result of the potato blight in Ireland in 1846 and 1847 and the granting of civic equality to Roman Catholics through the Catholic Emancipation Act of 1829. Finally, in 1850 the Catholic hierarchy was re-established in England during the papacy of Pius IX. Bishop Nicholas Wiseman was named cardinal and served as the archbishop of Westminster from 1850 to 1865, and the Roman Catholic Church became firmly established in England despite anti-Catholic cries of papal aggression.

The center of religious life in England was held by the Anglican Church, a body that increasingly incorporated many traditions as the nineteenth century unfolded. Among those who considered themselves to be Anglicans were Evangelicals, Christian Socialists such as F. D. Maurice and Charles Kingsley, and Anglo-Catholics. This latter wing of Anglicanism continued to function under the leadership of Edward Pusey and John Keble after the Oxford Movement, begun in 1833, paved the way for John Henry Newman's conversion to Rome in 1845 and Henry Edward Manning's conversion to Rome in 1851. To be sure, such conversions strengthened the position and the standing of the Roman Catholic Church in England throughout the remainder of the nineteenth century.

The Oxford Movement was one which originally saw the Church of England as the middle way between Protestantism and Roman Catholicism. However, many in the movement eventually saw the Roman Catholic Church as the true Church and eventually became Roman Catholics. Manning was made a cardinal in 1875 and Newman became a cardinal in 1879. Newman's influence came chiefly through his writings, especially those concerned with the viability and development of Christian doctrine. Manning's influence came as a result of his strong social conscience. He shared the common humanitarian and religious concerns for the plight of the poor and the laboring classes. He demonstrated an interest in both William Booth and The Salvation Army.

Victorian England was also influenced by Evangelicalism. A religious spirit commonly referred to as Evangelical pervaded Victorian England, such a spirit being traceable back to the preaching of John Wesley in the eighteenth century. "The direct descendants of Wesley formed the largest group outside the establishment."[11]

However, that Evangelical tradition, while Wesleyan in its inception, was far-reaching—it influenced not only the Methodists, but Congregationalists, Baptists, Quakers, and Anglicans as well. "In contemplating Victorian religion we need to remember The Salvation Army as well as Oxford University."[12] William Booth was both influenced by that Evangelical tradition, and became a sustainer of it.

The Evangelicals became known for a desire to save the souls of themselves and others, a pious moral existence which sometimes included total abstinence described gently by one author as "their want of appreciation of the spirit of cakes and ale"[13] and a strong social conscience. It was often the latter that drew the working classes to these dissenters. Thus there developed a distinct alliance between Evangelicals and the working classes, Evangelical chapels being filled with laborers. Evangelical influence began politically with the repeal of the Test Act in 1828. This opened up the possibility of political office for these Evangelicals, and such influence, combined with the rising humanitarian tide of Victorian England, would bring many needed reforms to Victorian society. In that way, Evangelicals would profoundly influence and shape the culture in which they found themselves.

Evangelicalism of the nineteenth century lost some support, especially among the intellectuals, over issues of Biblical inspiration and science. Evangelicals generally believed in the verbal inspiration of the Bible, and held to a literalistic interpretation of its message. For them, the scientific affirmations of Darwin and others were incompatible with the Biblical witness; scientific affirmations were untenable if they were in tension with the literal interpretation of all parts of Scripture. As the Victorian world developed after Darwin's *The Origin of Species* in 1859, the scientific community and the Evangelical community would grow further and further apart: increasing numbers of intellectuals would become anti-religious, with little attempt on the side of either community to strike a middle ground.

Such was the world that William Booth entered. He would be shaped by that world and would have his share of influence upon it. As Booth's social conscience developed through his own experiences, the environment of Victorian England would support the changes that he inaugurated, especially through the later ministry of The Salvation Army. Likewise, the religious nature of Victorian England, especially the Evangelical expression of it, would both nurture Booth on the one hand and allow him to express his Evangelical theology on the other hand. He would be both an expression of the nineteenth-century Evangelical tradition and a sustainer of it. His theology would reflect that interpretation as would the theology and the mission of his Christian Mission and Salvation Army.

The Life and Ministry of William Booth

William Booth was born on April 10, 1829 in Nottingham, England.[14] His father, from whom William Booth inherited a penchant for organization, was a nominal member of the Anglican Church, far more interested in business ventures than in religious ones. His mother, however, was a spiritually sensitive woman, pious and genuine, and she spiritually nurtured her son.

William Booth was baptized on April 12, 1829 at St. Stephen's Anglican Church near his home, and reared an Anglican by his parents. Two forces began to shape his thinking as he grew up in one of England's prominent industrial centers. One was Christianity, an inescapable force for anyone living at that place and at that time. However, Booth was not a person to embrace conventional forms for the sake of convenience. He looked upon Christianity, and especially the embodiment of Christianity, the Church, with a critical eye. Before the founding of The Christian Mission in 1865 and of The Salvation Army in 1878, Booth would become involved in several Christian denominations.

The second force was the intangible one of insufferable poverty and misery that he witnessed around him as a boy in Nottingham—that kind of suffering and deprivation which was one product of the Industrial Revolution. For a brief period of time the Chartists gained his attention, and he undoubtedly heard the speeches of Feargus O'Connor as he proclaimed the Chartist cause for the sake of the poor. However, even Booth's earliest sensitivities were religious, and in the earlier stages of his life he thought of the human condition in categories of sin and guilt. Therefore, he looked for religious solutions to human deprivation—solutions within orthodox Christianity.[15]

William Booth's search for some place of ministry led him out of Anglicanism and into the Methodist circles known as the Wesleyans. As will be noted in this study, William Booth, feeling encumbered by the formalism of Anglicanism, was attracted to the preaching of an American Methodist revivalist named James Caughey. Booth later traced his religious conversion to the influence of the Wesleyans, and he was nurtured by the preaching of James Caughey.[16]

In his active ministry before 1861, Booth moved through three separate denominations, after which he launched out on an independent ministry. By 1849, he was a licensed local preacher with the Wesleyans. He left the Wesleyans and, for a brief period of time, considered a ministry with the Congregationalists. However, the Calvinist doctrines of predestination and limited atonement drove him back to the Methodists with whom he felt theologically at home. He did not, however, return to the Wesleyans, but joined New Connexion Methodism, a group which had previously departed from the Wesleyans. He was trained for ministry by an eminent New Connexion Methodist minister named William Cooke.

Booth was an evangelistic preacher, and his desire for evangelistic work rather than the routine ministry of the parish brought him into confrontation with some of the leadership of New Connexion Methodism. He was neither by temperament nor by theology fitted for the work of the local preacher. He wanted to preach to the masses. He wanted to call the masses to repentance. William Booth was unhappy with the local ministry to which New Connexion Methodism insisted on confining him, and in 1861 there was a parting of the ways. He left New Connexion Methodism and spent the next four years in that endeavor to which he believed himself best suited: an independent, revivalist ministry.

In 1855, William Booth married Catherine Mumford, a woman who would become the most influential person in his life. She supported his leaving New Connexion Methodism, and she, along with William Booth, began in 1865 on Whitechapel Road in the East End of London what was later to be known as The Christian Mission. They concurred on two important matters: first, London was where they felt at home, and second, revivalist ministry to the masses of the poorest district in London was suited to their abilities. The Christian Mission evolved eventually into The Salvation Army in 1878, of which William Booth became the first General. However, Catherine Booth and the five daughters and three sons of the Booths were also integral to the work of The Christian Mission and The Salvation Army. All of the children became Salvation Army officers, and Catherine led The Salvation Army along with her husband but without any rank.

William Booth was an Evangelical. His loyalties were, nevertheless, not only to that broad Evangelical tradition of Victorian England. He thought of himself as not only Evangelical, but as Wesleyan. Beginning with his early associations with the Wesleyans in Nottingham under whose ministry he was saved, and continuing throughout his life, he had a great appreciation for John Wesley. In a letter to his son, Bramwell, on August 27, 1876, William Booth wrote:

> I have been reading Tyerman's Wesley in my illness and have, by comparing his (Wesley's) experience with my own, I think, derived some important lessons. One is that, under God, Wesley made Methodists not [only] by converting sinners, but by making well instructed saints. We must follow in his track, or we are a rope of sand. He laid as much stress on visiting the members privately, and in classes, as on preaching. Let us profit by the experience of those who have trod similar paths before us.[17]

Booth claimed that by the age of twenty he had become an admirer of John Wesley. He said this of himself:

> I worshipped everything that bore the name of Methodist. To me there was one God, and John Wesley was his prophet. I had devoured the story of his life. No human compositions seemed to me to be comparable to his writings, and to the hymns of his brother Charles, and all that was wanted, in my estimation, for the salvation of the world was the faithful carrying into practice of the letter and the spirit of his instructions.[18]

William Booth understood his inheritance from John Wesley to be twofold: first, he considered himself to be the theological heir of John Wesley, especially in his understanding of the doctrine of sanctification by grace. He was correct in this self-assessment, for he articulated the doctrine very much as Wesley had a century before. The characteristics of that doctrine will be examined in the first chapter.

Second, he considered himself to be the organizational heir of John Wesley. W. T. Stead noted this in comparing Booth and Wesley in his biography of William Booth. Stead wrote:

> Wesley understood the importance of organization. When he made an impression upon a man, he did not stop there. When he made a convert, he enlisted him as a recruit. He recognized the responsibility of leadership. He was not afraid to accept the duties of ruler. He framed orders and regulations, and when his followers criticized them, he wrote: "It is your duty to obey my rules, not to mend them."
>
> " ... Remember ... Wesley's success," has been the watchword of General Booth from the beginning. He has indeed remembered it. If The Salvation Army a hundred years after his death is not as vigorous and as solid an institution as the Methodist Churches, it will not be for want of organization.[19]

Not unexpectedly, Booth himself found support for this presupposition as did The Salvation Army. In an interesting letter to Catherine Booth in 1886 from Halifax, Booth wrote that "the most popular Methodist minister in St. John's, New Brunswick greeted me on Friday night on leaving for Halifax in the most respectful and affectionate manner, saying that next to John Wesley he hailed me benefactor to the world."[20] In an appeal to raise money for a missionary fund known as the Self-Denial Fund, *The War Cry* for September 28, 1895 stated that "Methodists of all shades will loyally support because in essence The Salvation Army is the work of John Wesley brought up to date."[21] However, a more objective source, G. M. Trevelyan in *English Social History*, gave some credence to these claims when he wrote that "The Salvation Army, founded by General Booth, brought the enthusiasm of conversion, after

Wesley's original fashion, to the Army of the homeless and unfed, to the drunkard, the criminal and the harlot."[22]

William Booth was a product of urban England. The cities of Nottingham and London were the cities that he knew best, and his theology took shape as he attempted to understand how he could reach the urban masses with the Gospel. Here was a basic religious question in Victorian England: could the Christian churches "adjust themselves to industrial revolution, speedy growth of population, and empire overseas?"[23]

The focus of this work is on the theology of William Booth, a theology with which he and his organizations became so inextricably united that it is impossible to write about one without writing about the other. William Booth committed himself fully to the work of those organizations until his death, or his "promotion to Glory" in Salvation Army terminology, on August 20, 1912. Therefore, to understand properly the place of William Booth and The Salvation Army in the nineteenth century and the beginning of the twentieth century, one must understand the developed theology of William Booth. To comprehend his theology is to understand the development of The Salvation Army from its Christian Mission days in 1865 to its organizational structure in 1912. Likewise, to know the theology of The Salvation Army is to know something of the theology of William Booth, for he, greatly influenced by several key people, increasingly provided the theological foundation, the theological drive, the theological legitimacy, and the theological vision for the movement.

Previous Treatments of William Booth

The previous treatments of Booth basically fall into two categories. There have been biographical works, but most of them are apologetics, and, while helpful in placing Booth in his historic context, fail to treat seriously the theology of Booth. Therefore, they are reductionist and inadequate in scope.

There have also been sociological appraisals of William Booth. These works concentrate on the "social work" of William Booth, but do not deal with the theology of William Booth, and therefore incorrectly see Booth only as a social activist of the latter part of the nineteenth century. While this perception is partially true, it does not nearly explain either the person or the movements which he and Catherine Booth established, and it fails to recognize that Booth's theology was absolutely essential to his work for the improvement of society. These sociological appraisals are likewise reductionist in scope, and are therefore inadequate.

Focus of This Study

The central assertion of this study is that the theology of William Booth changed. That change became evident after the founding of The Salvation Army in 1878. He developed a theology which evolved (1) from the use of individual categories, such as personal conversion and personal sanctification, to (2) the use of both individual and institutional categories such as corporate sanctification and the establishment of a physical kingdom of God on earth, with the most dramatic change being in his understanding of redemption.

It is hoped that this study will be beneficial to at least two groups of people. First, it should prove useful to The Salvation Army as an aid to self-understanding from a perspective now far removed from William Booth. The Salvation Army has only recently begun to gain a comprehension of and appreciation for the theology of William Booth, and the relationship of that theology to the organization.

This study will prove useful also to the wider scholarly world, and particularly to that world which is interested in nineteenth-century studies. William Booth played a significant role in the religious history of the nineteenth century, and the movements that he founded jointly with Catherine Booth also were important. How critical and vital those contributions were can be judged only by careful scrutiny by the objective scholar. However, that scholar is at a distinct disadvantage if he or she does not understand the theology of William Booth. This study will contribute to important sources of knowledge as it concentrates upon that theology.

Problems in Research

There were two major problems which this writer constantly encountered in his research. First, William Booth wrote voluminously, but there was a lack of precision in his writing. This is most evident in his use of various sources for his writing and preaching. He used these sources freely, and was not often precise in identifying them. He generally drew upon such sources either to derive his theology or to lend support to it. These sources were varied, as will be noted, but the most important and most quoted source for his theological positions was Scripture. He constantly quoted from the Bible and drew illustrations from it, which he was prone to apply to the ministry of The Christian Mission and later to The Salvation Army. The Bible was of central importance to William Booth, and he used it constantly.

He also used various other kinds of illustrations to support and give practical application to his theology. These illustrations were drawn from many sources, the most common of them being the history of the Church,[24] his own culture,[25] agrarian life,[26] nature,[27] or his own life, experiences and observations.[28] The latter provided Booth with his most common and most used source.

A third basic method of supporting his preaching and writing was the use of quotations. This area of study of the theology of William Booth presents the serious student with the most difficult research problems because Booth often quoted from someone without citing the source. Also, he sometimes referred to a quotation without identifying the author or source. The researcher of William Booth occasionally reads a quotation which was vaguely attributed to "a somewhat celebrated leader in the evangelistic world,"[29] or to "a celebrated Frenchman."[30] However, when he did quote accurately, and when he was careful to mention the sources of his quotations, those sources included as wide a selection as the Reverend Dr. Barry, Charles Booth, Bishop South, Charles Kingsley, John Fletcher, and Russell Lowell.[31]

Booth quoted most often from hymns, however. By far, his favorite writer of hymns was the prolific Charles Wesley. It is fair to say that William Booth was imbued with Wesleyan hymnody, and his quotations of Wesleyan hymns are found everywhere in his writings.[32] When not quoting from that source, he drew from a wide range of hymns, which were written both without and within The Salvation Army. He quoted, for example, from John Newton,[33] Isaac Watts,[34] Samuel H. Hodges,[35] William Pearson,[36] and Bramwell Booth.[37] He sometimes composed his own hymns.[38]

Lastly, Booth also made many passing references to people, often without benefit of footnote or direct quotation. These references were usually to such people in the history of the Church as Luther, Wesley, Whitefield,[39] or St. Francis of Assisi.[40] However, he was also prone to allude to people who either supported the work of The Salvation Army or were opposed to the work of the Army. For example, Professor Huxley, a critic of The Salvation Army, was one person to whom Booth made reference.[41]

Booth's lack of precision in giving references does make the study of his theology difficult at times, but there is a wealth of material to be considered when one is doing research of this nature. The primary sources, supplemented by the many biographies of William Booth and the many articles about William Booth, and augmented also by the works of people who were influential upon Booth, provide the material for this commentary.

A second major problem that was encountered in the research for this study was caused by Booth's lack of critical awareness of how theology is formulated or of how and why theology changes. He was not always aware of the forces which shaped his own theology or of the changes that were taking place in his theology. He was not a trained theologian, and so these details often escaped his attention.

Nor did Booth systematize his theology in any single volume or set of volumes. He preached and wrote on a wide range of theological topics, and his theology served him well for what he was striving to achieve in various stages of his life and ministry. However, for purposes of careful analysis, his theology has been structured into the categories which were most prevalent in the theological affirmations of Booth: the doctrine of revelation, the doctrine of God the Father, the doctrine of God the Son, the doctrine of God the Holy Spirit, the doctrine of the fall, the doctrine of the Church, the doctrine of redemption, and Christian ethics.

Overview of the Study

The chapters that follow seek to demonstrate the change that occurred in those themes so central in the theology of William Booth. Chapter I will deal with the early stage in the theology of Booth formulated during the time of his revivalist work and his leadership of The Christian Mission up to 1878. Chapter II will treat the change evident in the second stage in much of the theology of William Booth after the emergence of The Salvation Army in 1878.

Chapter III will examine the third stage in Booth's theology and his most significant change that he began to formulate in 1889 as his understanding of redemption moved beyond personal salvation alone to embrace more fully both personal and social salvation.

Stage One: The Ministry and Theology of William Booth to 1878

The early theology of William Booth was articulated primarily by the use of individual imagery and categories beginning at the time of his revivalist ministry and continuing throughout his time with The Christian Mission. An example of this is his emphasis on personal conversion and a resultant personal salvation. This will become clear as we concentrate on those doctrines that were most important in the early theology of Booth, beginning with his doctrine of revelation. However, in order to understand the context in which those doctrines were formulated, we will consider first the ministry of William Booth up to 1878.

The Ministry of William Booth

The Ministry of Revivalism

In 1849, William Booth moved to London to seek employment. By this time, however, his vocational sympathies were toward itinerant, revivalist preaching. After an association with the Wesleyans, and after considering a ministry with the Congregationalists, he finally associated with a movement called New Connexion Methodism from 1854 to 1861. His hopes were that he would be allowed to minister as an itinerant evangelist for that denomination, but the leadership of the denomination had other plans for Booth.

His departure from New Connexion Methodism was the result of a conflict over this very issue—the leadership wished to confine Booth to the parish ministry and refused to allow him the freedom needed for such revivalist preaching.

He left New Connexion Methodism in 1861, his resignation becoming effective in 1862, and until 1865 he did enjoy increasing popularity as a revivalist, conducting religious revivals for churches that were sympathetic with his mission. During the time of his preaching both within New Connexion Methodism and after leaving that denomination, Booth had one mission only— the saving of souls—and his success was measured by the number of converts. He was preaching to the masses, and it is true that his interest in the poor continued unabated, but he held that the greatest service that he could render to these people was not in the alleviation of their physical lot in life, but in reconciling them to God. His mission at this point was the single one of converting sinners and raising them up as saints. In retrospect nearly thirty years later, Booth willingly admitted to this single mission. In January, 1889, he wrote:

> The Bible and my own observation concurred in showing me that the highest service I could render to man, was to rescue him from this position of antagonism to the Divine Government. Alongside this aspect of his condition, any temporal modification of his lot appeared trivial—nay, almost contemptible. What were any of the sorrows of earth when compared with everlasting damnation—let man interpret that terrible doom however they would? And what were any of the joys of time when contrasted with the felicities which endure forever? Thus the desire to persuade men to be reconciled to God became henceforth the main propelling purpose of my life.[1]

The Founding of the East London Christian Revival Union

The Booths moved to London for one reason only—to accommodate Catherine so that she could accept a preaching engagement in the greater London area. She moved in with her parents in Brixton, and William went back up north to continue his preaching. William eventually moved back to London to join his wife and family, and began preaching in London. In 1865, William and Catherine Booth founded the East London Christian Revival Union which, after several name changes, would eventually be known as The Christian Mission.

William Booth was still a revivalist and evangelist, and his motivation was to preach to those whom neither church nor chapel were touching. He did not want to duplicate what was already being done, and the fledgling organization began in the East London (later referred to as the East End) in a place known as Mile End Waste. The preaching was done more in open-air services than indoor services after the fashion of John Wesley for the practical reason that those services were more attractive to people who would not darken the door of church or chapel.

There was a plan in place. Converts were to be instructed in the Christian faith and then sent to churches or chapels. The emphasis was on preaching the Gospel and converting sinners, and it is no surprise to find that Booth's rented mission centers at this time were called "Preaching Stations." The Christian Mission was to be an evangelical arm of the Church, and the Booths originally had no intention of launching a new denomination.

The Development of The Christian Mission

Refusal of many churches to admit back to membership people who were converted in The Christian Mission—added to a strong allegiance to the Booths by many of their followers, both converts and Christians who had joined The Christian Mission—culminated in The Christian Mission's increasing organization, administration, and authoritarian system. By 1868, a headquarters for The Christian Mission was located at 188 Whitechapel Road.

Finally in 1870, a constitution was established for The Christian Mission that was Methodist but with three distinctions:[2] much power was placed in the hands of the general superintendent, then William Booth himself; the equality of women in ministry was insisted upon; and office-holders in The Christian Mission had to be total abstainers from alcohol. In the meantime, The Christian Mission was in a growing stage, no longer renting its meeting places, but purchasing many of its meeting halls. *The Christian Mission Magazine* reported that by July of 1875, there were nineteen Christian Mission stations.[3] As of January of 1876, there were a total of thirty Christian Mission stations.[4] As will be noted in the next chapter, by 1878 that Christian Mission evolved into The Salvation Army, and a new denomination was on the scene.

The Theology of William Booth
The Doctrine of Revelation

The issue of revelation for Booth did not revolve around the place of natural revelation, or the distinction between general revelation and special revelation. His theological sympathies were all on the side of people like Luther who accentuated the propositional special revelation from God found in the Bible. Booth believed that God had disclosed Himself to people primarily through Jesus Christ, and that the authoritative witness to that fact was the Bible itself. He constantly referred to the Bible as the revelation from God to people, and he had a high view of the Bible. In his earlier years, his primary task was as evangelist and preacher, and his use of scripture was supportive of that task.

He was not a trained theologian and therefore did not concern himself with biblical criticism. He was not given to a disciplined analysis of biblical criticism, nor was he given to abstract philosophical or theological speculation. He had neither the trained mind nor the disposition of will for that level of theological discourse. However, two facts are worth remembering when dealing with Booth's approach to Scripture as revelation from God: first, his lack of concern for biblical criticism was something that he shared with others of similar Evangelical heritage of nineteenth-century England. "Evangelical piety remained Biblical and puritan. It had nothing to do with Biblical criticism, and remained conservative against doctrines of evolution or folklore in Genesis."[5]

Second, while recognizing his own deficiencies in his theological training, he did not share the anti-intellectual bias of some Evangelical biblicists in nineteenth-century England. He respected and admired those around him whose minds were trained in the finer, more abstract fields of theology, and his practical nature taught him to rely on those people when shaping his own theology. In a letter to his eldest son, Bramwell Booth, on August 27, 1876, he wrote, "Now you must have among other things a knowledge of systematic theology. You have felt lately your need here, and as a public man, probably a very public man, to hold your own with the preachers and the public you must have information and skill in controversial theology. "[6]

The revelation of God through Scripture was important to Booth. His high view of Scripture substantiated his view that Scripture provided the primary source for the doctrines that he espoused and the Christian life that he led. He believed the Bible was inspired by God and was therefore authoritative for the Christian. Precisely how the Bible was inspired by God would not be formulated until later. One close observer of Booth correctly stated that "He believed that the Bible was the inspired word of God: and in the Bible he found that the injunction to repent preceded the invitation to holiness. No one in his house questioned for a single moment, or in any respect, the truth of the Bible."[7]

In Booth's early years, the Bible was the primary source for his preaching of repentance and conversion. The Bible became, therefore, authoritative for his preaching, public speaking, and writing. As converts and others interested in his early preaching began to gather around him, he articulated this. In December 1868, in the *East London Evangelist*, he wrote: "In conclusion, it will be seen from the foregoing: .... That this is an unsectarian mission. Our creed is the Bible, our work is to publish the Gospel, and we welcome as co-workers all who hold the Word of God as the standard of faith and practice and whose hearts are in sympathy with revival work."[8]

In his early ministry, the Bible was his creed and for better or for worse, Booth then believed that the doctrines which he held were clear biblical truths. In *Religion for Every Day*, he stated that "the Bible is a valuable Book, because from it we learn all that we know about the Birth and Life, the Sufferings and Death, the Resurrection and Ascension of our Lord and Saviour Jesus Christ."[9] In that same work, he rehearsed the same theme in these words:

> It is the Bible that tells us of the merits of the Precious Blood of our dear Saviour, the possibilities of the Forgiveness of Sins, the Purification of our Hearts, the Protection of God, and the triumph of a dying hour. Of these blessed possibilities mankind would know nothing without the Bible.[10]

As will be noted in this chapter, one of the doctrines that was most important to this Wesleyan in these early years was the doctrine of sanctification. Not surprisingly, he believed that this doctrine was a biblical one, and he stated so. In *A Ladder to Holiness*, he wrote:

> From what I have read in the Bible, by what I heard from my comrades, and by the light God has given

me by His Holy Spirit in my own heart, I now see a
believe that it is possible for me to be delivered fr
all inward and outward sins, and that I can be m
holy in this life. I believe that I can, as the Scriptures
say, be cleansed from all filthiness of the flesh and of
the spirit, and be enabled to perfect holiness in the
fear of the Lord.[11]

While the Bible was the source of revelation in his early life,
he did not deny the importance and value of experience as both a
means of confirmation of what he learned from the Bible and as a
source of judgment for proper courses of action. A pragmatic man,
his range of experiences included those gained through family life,
religious training, reading, corresponding, preaching, some close
personal relationships with members of his family, with friends,
and with associates, and through his physical environment. However, his most important experience came through his observation
and analysis of what transpired in life around him every day. Booth
was, by his own constant admission, a person of common sense,
and he used that common sense to evaluate what he saw and heard
daily, to weigh and measure what he experienced against previously
held religious beliefs and convictions, to confirm what he learned
from Scripture, and to judge future courses of action for himself
and for others.

The relationship was, nevertheless, reciprocal—Booth's experiences also shaped his religious beliefs and convictions. As his
experiences changed, so did his theology, although not always
consciously. What he experienced during this time of his life
came largely through an active ministry of preaching. There were
important events in his early ministry that sometimes came to
him by a relationship with a denomination such as New Connexion Methodism, and that at other times were gleaned by private,
independent revivalist preaching. These events took on significance
as he reflected upon them with growing number of people around

him who both shared similar experiences and who developed similar theological sensitivities.

William Booth was accustomed to reflecting upon the importance of various experiences in his lifetime, and while the accuracy of his reflection in later years is debatable, the fact of his own high assessment of experience is undeniable. Speaking of the early years of his ministry, he observed that "during those years we have had to learn and unlearn a great deal, and to all the lessons of our experience the world is more than welcome."[12] As our study will show, this practical, experiential process of learning was continual for Booth. He stated:

> As I have already intimated, we do not pretend as yet to have finished our education. War is a wonderful schoolmaster, and he is unworthy of the name of soldier who does not continually seek to learn from foes as well as from friends, how most completely and rapidly to conquer.[13]

There are two aspects of the pragmatic Booth that must be mentioned, because these characteristics were important not only for the early Booth, but for the later Booth as well, and they were evident as Booth shaped his theology in every stage of his life. These two aspects were his optimism and his toleration. William Booth was a product of his age: he was a child of Victorian England, and the Victorian Age was characterized, among other things, by "the natural optimism of an age of progress."[14] That age was characterized by a general "feeling of struggle and pilgrimage,"[15] and Chadwick writes that this was exemplified by the popularity of John Bunyan's *Pilgrim's Progress*. Such optimism manifested itself both on a personal level of ultimate hope by "the contemplation of heaven,"[16] and on a societal level of ultimate hope, because "with this vision of a New Jerusalem went the religious drive to mend society."[17]

So it was with William Booth—he was an optimist on both the personal level and on the level of society. While he could not help but acknowledge both personal sin, and, ultimately, the power of evil, he did look forward, sometimes with eager anticipation, to the future. As his ministry developed, his optimism increased, and his final vision included a New Jerusalem.

This man reflected his Victorian heritage, secondly, in his toleration. Despite what Chadwick labels as "hooligan persecution"[18] against various dissenting groups during the Victorian Era (most notably the Primitive Methodists and The Salvation Army), and despite the strength of the Church of England during this time, the Victorians did eventually tolerate dissenting ideas and groups, and even moved beyond toleration to "an age of equality where speakers and writers sought to capture the public mind."[19]

Booth reflected this toleration. Even in his early ministry he was not a man given to criticism of other groups or of other parts of the Church. He was not a person who desired to enter into controversy with people. He was neither censorious toward the work of the Church, nor unsympathetic with the work of the Church. One place where Booth most dearly articulated this toleration in this early phase of his ministry was in his "Dedication" of the first issue of *The East London Evangelist*, the earliest publication of The Christian Mission. There he stated:

> To all earnest laborers in the Lord's vineyard: to all those who, obedient to the Master's command, are simply, lovingly, and strenuously seeking to rescue souls from everlasting burnings, through His own precious blood, who, believing in the promise of the Father, are seeking with strong cries and tears for a mighty outpouring of the Holy Spirit to stem the rising tide of error and superstition, break up the slumbers of the professing church, arrest the attention of a dying world, and clothe the religion of Jesus with its primitive simplicity, fervour and energy—to such belonging to

whatever division of the Church of the living God, or
engaged in whatever department of Christian effort,
with yearnings of deep sympathy we dedicate the "East
London Evangelist" wishing abundance of peace and
prosperity in the Master's name.[20]

The Doctrine of God the Father

We turn now to a second doctrine that he assumed came primarily
from Scripture and secondarily from his observation of the natural
world, and was confirmed by his own experience, the doctrine
of God the Father. This was not admittedly the most important
doctrine for Booth, and his reflections upon God usually turned
quickly to God the Son or to God the Holy Spirit. He did not possess Calvin's consciousness of God the Father or His providence.
Booth's understanding of God the Father was informed not by
philosophical arguments for the existence of God, but from his
reading in the Bible about God and from his understanding of
the relationship of God to His created order. While his doctrine
of God the Father was not paramount, some sense of order in
Booth caused him to articulate this doctrine immediately after his
doctrine of Scripture when he set forth the initial cardinal doctrines for The Christian Mission. This occurred formally first in
the minutes of the first Conference of The Christian Mission held
in 1870. Following the doctrine on Scripture, the doctrine on God
the Father read thus:

> We believe that there is only one God who is infinitely per-
> fect, the Creator, Preserver, and Governor of all things.[21]

While God is not referred to here specifically as God the
Father, it is clear in two distinct ways that the reference is to
the first person of the Trinity. First, the functions that are
assigned to God in this statement are primarily functions of
God the Father (e.g., that of creation). Second, the context of the

orth in the minutes of The Christian
m that this is a reference to God the
tement there was a doctrine on the
ɔws:

ɛ are three persons in the Godhead,
, and the Holy Spirit, undivided in
al in power and glory, and the only
ligious worship.[22]

Christological statement. Thus there was
hristian Mission doctrines, leading from
ty, to God the Son, and so forth.

ɔctrine of God the Son

There is no evidence that William Booth, in contrast to his mentor, John Wesley, was knowledgeable about the early Church fathers and the Christological or trinitarian controversies which spanned hundreds of years and the first seven councils of the Church. Just as there was an assumption about the Trinity, so there was an assumption about the two natures of Jesus Christ. The relationship between the two natures was articulated as part of the initial doctrines of The Christian Mission in 1870 in the following way:

> We believe that in the person of Jesus Christ the divine
> and human natures are united, so that He is truly and
> properly God and truly and properly man.[23]

Here the matter rested. The intricacies of the doctrines of the Trinity and of Christ escaped Booth's notice as did the relationship of the two doctrines, due primarily to his lack of formal theological training.

His interest in the doctrine of Jesus Christ was practical and pastoral, and his concentration was less on the person of Jesus Christ than on the work of Jesus Christ. However, even here, although showing some familiarity with the theological language of atonement, Booth lacked both an historical and a critical approach to a subject, which had been a major theological concern for the Church since the first century. He showed no familiarity with the range of images of the atonement from Augustine's Pauline emphasis carried on by Luther, to Anselm's substitutionary emphasis, to Abelard's relationship of atonement to incarnation.

Neither did he demonstrate a clear perception of the development of the doctrine from the Old Testament to the New Testament on to the nineteenth century. He did not enter into debate about the relationship of atonement and salvation, and did not make fine distinctions between these two doctrines. Generally, he referred to atonement and salvation synonymously, and often referred to salvation in the Pietistic imagery of the new birth.

Herein lies a recurring chief weakness with Booth who willingly entered the theological dialogue by his preaching and teaching: he was content to believe that his understanding of atonement (and his other doctrines) came directly from the Bible and that what he was preaching and teaching was concomitant with the complete word of God in Scripture. He often demonstrated a lack of perception concerning the development of a doctrine within the Bible itself, or the complicated and various means used in the Bible to elucidate a particular doctrine. He likewise demonstrated a lack of perception about the development of a doctrine within the history of the Church, or, similarly, the various and complicated means used to explain a doctrine.

Finally, he did not demonstrate understanding of how his own theological background, culture, or environment shaped and defined the very language he used to articulate, for example, the atonement. In this way, he was different from his principal theological mentor, John Wesley. While Wesley was obviously important to Booth, Booth saw Wesley in a limited way—as evangelist, preacher, and organizer. He did not comprehend the whole Wesley. He failed to understand precisely how Wesley arrived at his doctrinal formulations, and he failed also to incorporate into his own theology a knowledge of the history of theology.

Positively, however, Booth was being faithful to his own stated tasks: he was an evangelist, addressing the masses in ways that both he and they understood. He never laid claim to formal theological education, and the doctrines that he espoused functioned well for him as preacher to the masses. He had a high view of the person and work of Jesus Christ, and reflected the observation that "the theology of the later Victorians moved a little away from the atonement towards the incarnation."[24] The emphasis on both the atonement and the incarnation was present in Booth's theology, but the earlier Booth concentrated more on the atonement as a resolution to his understanding of personal sin and guilt. The later Booth concentrated more on the incarnation, especially in his insistence that Jesus Christ was the great model of the conquering Lord, and that He was still present with His people, giving them strength to conquer oppressive evil. Victorians were, after all, "conscious of Jesus the man. They therefore realized the possibility of a literal, i.e., a human, imitation of Him in his humanity. *The Imitation of Christ* was a book that sold in increasing numbers, and the idea of imitation became prominent in sermons."[25]

Booth's understanding of the atonement was practical and pastoral: he believed that people needed to be at one again with God since the fall. He was sure that this could not be accomplished by people because of their state of rebellion against God. Therefore, God came to earth in the person of Jesus Christ to accomplish atonement in two ways: first, by dying on the cross in the place of all sinners, Jesus Christ satisfied God's demand for justice and demonstrated God's love. In this dimension of the atonement, the emphasis was upon Jesus' death and upon the necessity of each person to repent of sins and believe on Jesus Christ.

In addition to this, by being raised from the dead, Jesus Christ conquered such unholy alliances as evil and death, and initiated the redemption of the whole world from the jaws of evil and death. In this dimension of the atonement, the emphasis was upon Jesus' resurrection and upon the necessity of believers taking the side of the conquering Christ in the work of redemption of the world.

Therefore, for William Booth the dimensions and dynamics of salvation were both personal and societal. However, the personal element was predominant in the early Booth. That was true because his view of the fall at that time was limited principally to personal sin and guilt. He would later broaden his understanding of the fall to include societal evil, and then his view of the atonement would widen and complement his understanding of incarnation. It was true also because the ministry of the early Booth was limited to preaching without the benefit of the organization, which he would later found. As his movement developed to include social salvation as well as personal salvation, his view of the atonement would broaden.

However, in this early phase of his ministry, the primary emphasis relating to the work of Jesus Christ was this: the individual is saved by the work of Christ on the cross through faith. "If the past merits condemnation, repent honestly and fully before God, lay aside every weight and the sin which doth most easily beset you; and seek through the ever availing blood of the atonement, a renewed sense of the divine favor."[26] In a letter to Catherine Mumford on November 17, 1852, William Booth wrote about the nature of faith in this way: "The great plan of salvation is, ceasing from making efforts to make unto yourself a righteous character, and sinking helpless into the arms of Christ, and accepting Full Salvation, a pure heart, and all the blessings of the New Covenant by faith."[27]

The Doctrine of God the Holy Spirit

Equally important for Booth was the doctrine of the Holy Spirit. As has been mentioned, the precise nature and inter-relationship of the Trinity eluded Booth, and apart from affirming the three persons in the Godhead, he did not attempt to elaborate any further upon the relationship of the Holy Spirit to the Father and the Son. He was unaware of heresies associated with the Holy Spirit in the early Church propagated by people like Montanus and Macedonius, but demonstrated a general sense that the person and work of the Holy Spirit had often been neglected by the Church throughout its history, only to be emphasized again by John Wesley.

Like his doctrine of Christ, his emphasis was on the work of the Holy Spirit, and only secondarily on the person of the Holy Spirit. In fact, while he elaborated at times on the person of Jesus Christ, he did very little to identify the person of the Holy Spirit. There was an attempt in the formulation of the doctrines of The Christian Mission to articulate the person of God the Father and the person of God the Son. However, there was no equal or similar doctrinal attempt to understand the person of the Holy Spirit. For Booth, the Holy Spirit was comprehended almost totally by the manifestations of His work, that being the work of sanctification in the believer. That "privilege of all believers to be wholly sanctified, and that their whole spirit and soul and body 'may be preserved blameless unto the coming of our Lord Jesus Christ' (I Thessalonians 5:23),"[28] became central to that theology. This theological expression was valuable in Booth's early years because it was the final solution to his understanding of personal sin. It continued to be important to Booth in his later years because it was inextricably related to his eschatology—to his understanding of the kingdom of God and the ultimate conquest of not only personal sin, but of systemic evil.

The Doctrine of the Fall

It is necessary to move to Booth's theology of the fall, an issue to which he gave much attention during this early theological stage. As revivalist and preacher, he made anthropological pronouncements that reflected his understanding of people basically as sinners in rebellion against God and in need of salvation. He spent little time on the doctrine of creation, on the initial innocence and blessedness of people at creation, or on the uniqueness of people from the rest of creation because of the image of God in them. He dealt with reality as he found it and as he interpreted it, and he sought theological explanations for the sinful human nature, which he encountered both in himself and in the people to whom he preached.

Above all, he sought biblical imagery that would help to explain the sinful condition of all humanity. He nowhere demonstrated familiarity with the arguments since Augustine regarding the *imago dei* and how much of that image is lost or retained after the fall. He often referred to total depravity, not so much to conform with some Reformation doctrine of the present state of the image of God in people, but to accentuate the radically sinful state in people—that state of rebellion against God. His experience confirmed his interpretation of the Bible, and he certainly found supporting evidence in nineteenth-century Victorian England to substantiate his claim that people are sinners. He found this evidence also in his own nature.

Booth did not clearly define the relationship between original sin and the fall. The statement of The Christian Mission in 1870, in which there was no mention of original sin, read:

> We believe that our first parents were created in a state
> of innocence, but by their disobedience they lost their
> purity and happiness; that, in consequence of their fall,
> all men have become sinners, totally depraved, and as
> such are justly exposed to the wrath of God.[29]

The exact means of consequence was not spelled out, and no statement was made regarding the Augustinian notion of the biological transmission of original sin, or the Reformation notion of Adam as the representative of the human race with its emphasis on the corruption of human nature. Booth was never precise here, and he spoke and wrote about the fall rather than original sin. That fall, as will be noted again, was the result primarily of human free choice in rebellion against God.

He was not, however, Pelagian. He believed that all people participate in the fall. He believed that all people choose to sin, and he held that this was taught in the Bible and confirmed by his own experience. Booth was in keeping with Wesleyan theology in his emphasis on the fall, but certainly out of harmony with nineteenth-century evolutionary thought that stressed, not the fall from a higher and nobler order, but the progression of humanity from a lower order.

Much of nineteenth-century theology certainly reflected this in espousing that people were essentially good, and had the potential to progress to a better state.

Booth did not emphasize original sin in the same way that Wesley did as the latter built upon Luther and Calvin. Nor did he attempt to define, as Wesley did, the relationship of original sin and the fall. Like Wesley, however, his interests were largely pastoral—he believed that people were sinners by choice, he preached repentance from sin, and he established people in the Christian faith. However, his ministry was largely to adults, and he assumed a certain amount of responsibility in most adults. The issues of mentally impaired adults and children, and the Augustinian notion of washing away of original sin by baptism, along with the idea of infant baptism for that reason, did not enter into Booth's theologizing on the fall. Thus in his early ministry he understood the fall primarily within the category of personal sin, personal rebellion against God, and therefore the central emphasis of this active ministry was that of calling people to repentance. Booth believed in the fall, and he envisioned human beings in their state of rebellion against God. Harold Begbie, the biographer chosen by the Booth family and one of Booth's most competent biographers, wrote:

> For William Booth was always struggling against the two antithetical qualities of his nature—a loving, warm-hearted, generous sympathy, and a rigorous, unsparing, religious honesty. At one moment he hungered to see only the good in human nature; at the next, he was stung to a passionate indignation by its badness—its deadness to God. In his generous moods he would speak with a broad and embracing charity, a large and kindly tolerance of mankind; in his moods of realism and intellectual honesty he could not find words sharp and piercing enough for the evil of the world.[30]

This young preacher was confirmed by both Scripture and his own experience that basically, although he would have it otherwise, people "left to themselves, could not be good."[31] Because in this time of his ministry his imagery of the fall was in personal categories, the basic sin of the fall upon which he concentrated was the sin of selfishness. The fall of people from God was radical—it was complete and entire. He stated:

> The condition is thorough-entire. In his flesh there dwelleth no good thing. We need not quote from Scripture; we know that its testimony, no less than our experience and observation, describes and demonstrates the fact that man in his natural state is totally gone away from God, and that from the crown of his head to the sole of the foot he is all wounds and bruises and putrifying sores.[32]

Two important aspects of Booth's doctrine of the fall must be stressed here. First, people have been left with two clear choices. They must choose either to repent of their sins and return to God, or they choose to remain in their sins—in their willful and rebellious transgressions of God's law. After making the choice, people must live with the consequences of their choices and actions. Those consequences manifest themselves both in this world and in the next. Of that, Booth was sure. While the freedom to make those choices had been lost at the fall, through God's prevenient grace such freedom of choice was restored in all humanity.

In addition, it must be reiterated that William Booth was here dealing primarily with personal sin and guilt. This is meaningful because it sheds light on Booth's doctrine of redemption at this point of his ministry. In that doctrine, he concentrated on justification by faith and sanctification by faith as the antidotes to personal sin. His doctrine of redemption consisted of the resolution of the problem of that personal sin that Scripture and his own experience had illuminated.

The Doctrine of the Church

However, before moving to the doctrine of redemption, mention must be made of Booth's doctrine of the Church in these early years. As would be expected, his doctrine of the Church at this period of independent evangelistic preaching was not as clearly developed as in his later ministry when he had established a growing movement. In those later years, his organizational and institutional loyalties would play an important role in shaping his theology of the Church.

When dealing with the doctrine of the Church, Booth did not formally define the Church in ways that were crucial since Augustine. He did not make a clear distinction between the invisible Church and the visible Church. He did not have a doctrine of the Church that could be identified as Augustinian or Calvinistic or Lutheran. Nonetheless, informally he did have a notion of the invisible Church (although he did not use that term) as consisting of those who had been justified by faith. He certainly believed that his early Christian Missioners could be so construed as members of the Church by that definition.

Second, he had a notion of the visible Church as those who bore witness to their justification by preaching or by other significant means. He therefore was insistent on relating Church and mission. The Church may be contained in all denominations. Booth was not a twentieth-century fundamentalist, intent on writing off whole denominations. He would have no part of that. However, the Church was not synonymous with any denomination—one did not have to be a part of an existing denomination in order to be assured that he or she was part of the Body of Christ on earth. That was confirmed in both William and Catherine Booth upon their departure from New Connexion Methodism.

The Lutheran, Calvinist, and Anglican identification of the visible Church with the lawful celebration of the sacraments was never included in the identification of the visible Church for Booth, although the sacraments of baptism and the Lord's Supper were observed in The Christian Mission, with The Salvation Army eventually embracing a non-practicing position. Booth was therefore able to become non-practicing without having to re-interpret his doctrine of the Church.

Booth was not myopic. He never fell into the trap of identifying his movement with the whole Church. He did affirm, however, that his preaching, The Christian Mission, and The Salvation Army constituted part of the universal Church, and as military imagery came to the fore, Booth sharpened his analogy of The Salvation Army as a military branch of the Church.

However, the precise problem of defining the Church is not clear in Booth's writings. A few facts are evident: Booth was tolerant of other Christian traditions. He avoided defining the Church negatively by excluding one denomination or another. He never demonstrated a strong anti-Catholic or anti-Anglican bias, and would not have been willing to claim divine insight into the question of who, precisely, belonged to the Body of Christ. For him the Church was fundamentally the body of believers who were saved by grace through faith. They demonstrated this fact by bearing witness to it by word of mouth and by good works.

At this point, there were two clear characteristics that governed Booth's doctrine of the Church. First, because he certainly recognized the importance of the work of the Church and knew the significance of the denominations that he had left, he had to affirm that his early work was also the work of the Church universal. This was so because this work was divinely ordained by God. That ordination, that blessing, gave authority to Booth's early work and to his earliest independent organization known as The Christian Mission. As expected, that sense of divine sanction developed as The Christian Mission and The Salvation Army grew, and, for Booth at least, would legitimate the very existence of those organizations as part of the universal Church on earth. "God and you! There is no battalion of devils out of hell to-day," he wrote in 1875, "that can defeat you! There is no mob of bad men that can stop your way! No dead, inert church can keep you back! No iron-clad soul can altogether resist your words-God and you!"[33]

A second characteristic had to do with the actual work of the Church on earth. Booth's lifetime contention was that the basic work of the Church was redemption. Redemption would become a central theme in the theology of William Booth, and in this phase of his life the work of redemption consisted primarily in calling people to repentance and raising up saints. That was one sign that the Church was the true Church, and that was manifested primarily in preaching and otherwise bearing witness to the Gospel. In a "Letter from William Booth to the Brethren and Sisters Labouring for Jesus in Connection with the Dunedin Hall Christian Mission, Edinburgh," Booth wrote that "the work in which you are engaged is the most important that can engage the attention or call forth the energies of any being."[34]

The Doctrine of Redemption

As has been mentioned, Booth's reading of the Bible, confirmed by his experience, drew him in his early ministry continually to an understanding of personal sin and personal rebellion against God. He preached to sinners, and he called them to repentance. His doctrine of redemption was so critical at this point because it was the answer to the fall, to personal sin. And because his conception of the fall was cast in personal categories, his doctrine of redemption was articulated in personal categories.

Redemption begins with justification by faith in Christ. Those who believed were pardoned of their sins and were at one with God. However, the juridical language was less significant in Booth's preaching than the language of salvation and the language of rescue. Nevertheless, he was not consistent in his analogies, and, basically, his preaching consisted of these steps: pointing out people's personal sin and rebellion against God, calling them to repentance, and finally calling them to believe in Christ, or to be rescued from the waters in which they were perishing. They would then be reconciled with God, at one with God, or saved and safely on the shore of God's new kingdom. Atonement, reconciliation, redemption, and salvation were used synonymously by Booth, and the images which controlled these concepts were used interchangeably.

However, neither in his early ministry nor in his later ministry was justification by faith, nor personal salvation, the only focal point in Booth's doctrine of redemption. Booth was Wesleyan, and as such he believed that the doctrine of sanctification by faith was also central to the doctrine of redemption. As one author has noted, in the early years of the *East London Evangelist*, an explanation "that much space was to be devoted to the topic of personal holiness was accompanied by a statement that the importance of this theme could not possibly be overrated."[35] In an August 1877 article of a later magazine of The Christian Mission appropriately called *The Christian Mission Magazine*, William Booth stated that "holiness to the Lord is to us a fundamental truth: it stands to the forefront of our doctrines."[36]

The doctrine of sanctification was a central doctrine in the teaching and preaching of John Wesley, and the Methodists had become known for their explanation of the doctrine. John Wesley identified sanctification in this way:

> And at the same moment that we are justified, yea, in that very moment, sanctification begins. In that instant we are born again, born from above, born of the Spirit: there is a real as well as a relative change. We are inwardly renewed by the power of God. We feel "the love of God shed abroad in our heart by the Holy Ghost which is given unto us;" producing love to all mankind and more especially to the children of God: expelling the love of the world, the love of pleasure, of ease, of honour, of money, together with pride, anger, self-will, and every other evil temper; in a word, changing the earthly, sensual, devilish mind, into "the mind which was in Jesus Christ."
>
> From the time of our being born again, the gradual work of sanctification takes place. We are enabled "by the Spirit" to "mortify the deeds of the body," of our evil nature; and as we are more and more dead to sin, we are more and more alive to God. We go on from grace to grace, while we are careful to "abstain from all appearance of evil," and are "zealous of good works," as we have opportunity, doing good to all men; while we walk in all His ordinances blameless, therein worshipping Him in Spirit and in truth; while we take up our cross, and deny ourselves every pleasure that does not lead us to God.

> It is thus that we wait for entire sanctification; for
> a full salvation from all our sins—from pride, self-will,
> anger, unbelief; or, as the Apostle expresses it, "go on
> unto perfection." But what is perfection? The word has
> various senses: here it means perfect love. It is love
> excluding sin; love filling the heart, taking up the whole
> capacity of the soul. It is love "rejoicing evermore, pray-
> ing without ceasing, in everything giving thanks."[37]

Here is where Booth best understood John Wesley. Here he
embraced Wesley fully: along with justification comes initial sanctification; people grow in God's grace until, by faith, they receive
perfect love, after which they continue in their Christian growth.
This was distinct from both the monastic notion of perfection by
separation from the world and good works, and from the Calvinist
notion of sanctification as that which is continual after justification
and made complete at death. Booth wanted to make saints as well
as convert sinners.

This was also his doctrine of sanctification in these early years:
holiness, perfect love, the pure heart. It was a doctrine that in no
way, Booth taught, diminished the importance and the greatness
of the doctrine of justification by faith. But sanctification was as
crucial to Booth's theology as justification because it was his final
answer, his final solution, to personal sin and guilt.

He was sure that sanctification was a second, definite work
of grace in the heart of the believer. He was convinced that this
work, this pure heart, this baptism of the Holy Spirit, was the first
"great need"[38] of believers, and he taught that, just as justification
was appropriated by faith, so sanctification was also appropriated
by faith. He asked, "If you think with me, will you not tarry for it?
Offer yourselves to God for the fullness."[39]

Also, Booth was aware that some may oppose the doctrine.
However, he warned his readers, "Don't doubt or fear, or reason;
but steadily believe, though the fearful flesh, a lying devil, an infidel
world, and cold-hearted professors all suggest that it is impossible

that God should, according to His unfailing promise, cleanse you from all unrighteousness and preserve you blameless, and fill you with all the divine fullness."[40]

Because sanctification was at the core of redemption at this early stage, Booth was constantly engaged in attempts to define the doctrine, not in order to articulate fine, sophisticated nuances of the doctrine, but to make it meaningful and practical in the lives of those to whom he preached and wrote. The believer accepted the gift of sanctification by faith, but who was the giver of that gift? Booth was not clear about that, although the primary agent of sanctification was certainly the Holy Spirit. However, holiness was also the work of God the Father and God the Son. Booth thought interchangeably of the agency of holiness, and did not limit that work to the Holy Spirit alone.

The earliest formulation of the doctrine of sanctification is found in the minutes of the first Conference of The Christian Mission in 1870. The ninth doctrine articulated the meaning of holiness, and a Christian Mission Conference of 1876 went on to clarify further that meaning.[41] In an address on holiness to the 1877 Conference of The Christian Mission, William Booth claimed that the power of evil still existed in the soul of the believer after justification by faith, even though that power was diminished. But, claimed Booth, God has taken evil from the throne of the soul in the act of sanctification and given the believer power over evil. "He is no longer under sin but under grace."[42] Deliverance is partial in the act of justification, but complete in the act of sanctification. "Not only can Agag be taken captive, but hewn in pieces. Sin can not only be held in bondage, but destroyed."[43]

Booth employed various imagery to explain the doctrine, and as his theology developed he became more articulate about the doctrine. He encountered criticism about the doctrine, but criticism often had the opposite effect from its stated purpose—it forced Booth to articulate the doctrine further and clarify his position. Because Booth was convinced that the doctrine of sanctification was biblical doctrine, he insisted that it be taught and believed by his followers.[44]

Analogous to his doctrine of unlimited atonement, Booth taught also that every believer could be sanctified. The possibility of sanctification was open to all; however, only those who believed enjoyed the reality of it. Once enjoyed, one would have assurance of the experience by the witness of the Holy Spirit. However, as with justification, one must be sure not to backslide from the experience by either continual rebellion against God or by a continual lack of trust that God will persist in working in the heart. The best way to maintain the assurance of sanctification was to confess it openly and often in public.

Booth's Wesleyan heritage and upbringing was evidenced in his understanding of this doctrine in his early ministry. Because he was convinced of the importance of this doctrine, even at this early stage, and because he believed that it was vital to proclaim this doctrine, he taught that the desire for sanctification needed to be created in people. It was his experience that many Christians did not feel the need for sanctification, and early in his preaching career he believed that this was true for two reasons: the desire for holiness had not been properly created in people, and people had not clearly understood what the doctrine of sanctification entailed.[45]

It is beyond doubt that Booth's preaching in his early ministry entailed the preaching of the doctrine of sanctification. This became true, later, for preachers in The Christian Mission and in The Salvation Army. Robert Sandall, in the second volume of The History of The Salvation Army, was correct in his assessment of this matter when he wrote:

> …William and Catherine Booth when stationed at Gateshead (1860) decided it was incumbent on them to set forth the doctrine definitely and regularly. In the first number of The East London Evangelist (1868) William Booth further declared that the importance of

the doctrine could not be over-estimated, and till his promotion to Glory (1912) placed it on the forefront of his teaching wherever he went. Bramwell Booth's first important step in public service was to conduct weekly at the Whitechapel headquarters holiness meetings, the influence of which reached to the ends of the earth.[46]

At the Conference of The Christian Mission in January, 1877, Booth himself stated:

Holiness to the Lord is to us a fundamental truth; it stands to the forefront of our doctrines. We write it on our banners. It is in no shape or form an open debatable question as to whether God can sanctify wholly, whether Jesus does save his people from their sins. In the estimation of The Christian Mission that is settled forever, and any evangelist who did not hold and proclaim the ability of Jesus Christ to save His people to the uttermost from sin and sinning I should consider out of place amongst us.[47]

Such preaching was a call away from the power of personal sin and toward the possibility of personal saintliness. Booth's earliest concerns, after leaving New Connexion Methodism, were not for organizing a movement, nor for preserving loyalty to an organization through the doctrine of sanctification, nor for envisioning a universal redemptive ministry for such an organization. However, these kinds of loyalties became important for the later Booth, and even as early as 1869 we can see Booth beginning to articulate the doctrine of sanctification as having importance beyond that of personal holiness. He began then to understand sanctification as having something to do with the redemption of the world. Believing that "spiritual work can only be done by those who possess spiritual power,"[48] he wrote the following in *The East London Evangelist* in April 1869 in his "Letter From William Booth To The Brethren and

Sisters Labouring for Jesus in Connection with the Dunedin Hall Christian Mission, Edinburgh":

> But how much more might be done had you all received this Pentecostal baptism in all its fulness. If every soul were inflamed, and every lip touched, and every mind illuminated, and every heart purified with the hallowed flame. O what zeal, what self-denial, what meekness, what boldness, what holiness, what love would there not be? The whole city would feel it. God's people in every direction would catch the fire, and sinners would fall on every side. Difficulties would vanish, devils be conquered, infidels believe, and the glory of God be displayed. As it is written, Every valley would be filled, and every mountain and hill be brought low, and the crooked would be made straight, and the rough ways be made smooth, and all flesh would see the salvation of God.[49]

And still later to his growing number of Christian Missioners in 1877 he said that "the full equipment and qualification and guarantee of success in the great work of pulling down the kingdom of Satan, and establishing and extending the kingdom of God, is: Brethren be ye holy, and be holy now."[50]

In his early theology, however, personal categories were dominant—personal sin, personal salvation, personal holiness, personal witness. Therefore, one finds little of his theology expressed in corporate images of systemic evil, social salvation, or institutional sanctification.

Christian Ethics

All good theology ends in ethics, and in this early state of his ministry Booth was accustomed to formulating ethical principles from Scripture. His ethics at this time reflected the personal categories into which his wider theological concerns were cast. Booth assumed that Christians would lead lives of personal piety, virtue and honesty, and that these characteristics would manifest themselves in appropriate outward actions in the home, market, work place, and meeting hall. Later, as his theology included corporate images and categories, his Christian ethics reflected not only personal ethics, but also those ethics which would have social ramifications and would ultimately be manifested in a whole redeemed just society. For the present, however, Booth's central mission was to participate in the redemption of souls, and holy living sufficed as a sign of one's redemption. Changes, both doctrinal and ethical, will be demonstrated in later chapters of this study.

Stage Two: The Ministry and Theology of William Booth to 1889-1890

The change in William Booth's theology that came after the founding of The Salvation Army in 1878 was articulated not only in individual categories, but in institutional categories as well. An example of this would be Booth's doctrine of institutional sanctification that complemented his doctrine of personal sanctification. Such change was evident in most of the later theology of Booth, and this chapter will deal with that later theology as it reflected such change.

The Ministry of William Booth

Transition from The Christian Mission to The Salvation Army

As military language became common within the ranks of The Christian Mission, as Christian Missioners began to use titles or ranks for themselves, and as Booth began to be referred to as General rather than as general superintendent, The Christian Mission evolved into The Salvation Army in 1878 when the title was first used. The evolution was a natural one, and the British penchant for uniforms, titles, and public ceremony came to the service of this newly founded organization—ordained ministers became officers with ranks, laypersons became soldiers, all wore uniforms, bands were formed to attract people to the open-air services and to provide music for the indoor meetings, and public meetings and marches became commonplace in England.

The *Christian Mission Magazine* for September 1878, reported that: "The Christian Mission has met in Congress to make War. It has glorified God for the conquests of 1877-1878. It has organized a salvation army [sic] . . . to carry the blood of Christ and the fire of the Holy Ghost into every corner of the world."[1] In explaining "Our New Name" in *The Salvationist* for January 1, 1879, William Booth wrote: "We are a salvation people—this is our specialty—getting saved and keeping saved, and then getting somebody else saved, and then getting saved ourselves more and more until full salvation on earth makes the heaven within, which is finally perfected by the full salvation without, on the other side of the river."[2]

The Organization of The Salvation Army

The authoritarian structure of The Christian Mission served this fledgling movement well, and a hierarchy was developed that characterizes The Salvation Army even to this day. William Booth became the first General of The Salvation Army, and the ordained ministers, known as officers, were given ranks. The highest rank was that of commissioner and the rank of the newly commissioned officer was that of lieutenant. Within the spectrum the most common ranks included those of captain, major, and colonel.

As the movement developed, the ranking system became more fixed. Patterned after the British military system, the ranking system and structure that developed within The Salvation Army served at least three functions: it guaranteed allegiance to William Booth who was the first General; it provided a unified vision and goal for the members of the organization, the final direction being the establishment of the kingdom of God; and it sustained the existence of the movement.

Booth's primary social involvement was in The Salvation Army, and it is important to understand the relationship between him and the Army. Once The Salvation Army was founded, he was not one Salvationist among many. He was the autocratic head of what would become an international Army. In order to elucidate the relationship of the person and the movement, a brief discussion of the authoritarian structure of The Salvation Army will be helpful.

Booth had discovered experientially that he was suited temperamentally to the establishment and maintenance of an authoritarian structure, and those around him, drawn by his charismatic personality and his organizational abilities, reinforced this thinking. Therefore, The Salvation Army assumed such a structure.

One aspect of his authoritarian organization and control, for which Booth was severely criticized, was the role which he established for himself. This general superintendent of The Christian Mission and later General of The Salvation Army was an autocratic figure. He was by nature a despiser of committees, and he was committed to the principle that an Army for God needed one leader—one General. It was suggested, without grounds, that Booth consciously established the structure of The Salvation Army on the model of papal authority of the Roman Catholic Church. Some writers have raised the question as to whether Booth was inspired by papal autocracy.[3] In any case, Booth held that all Salvationists "must be consecrated and yielded up to the carrying out of the plans and purposes the Army adopts for the salvation of the world."[4] And one principle basic to that consecration was obedience to the General, "implicit obedience."[5]

In spite of secessions from The Salvation Army by members of his own family,[6] Booth never wavered on the issue of "voluntary subjection to an absolute authority."[7] In fact, his resolve to maintain this structure was strengthened throughout his long life and career. His apologetic for such autocracy was that no one needed to remain in the Army "a day longer than he pleases."[8] However, while a person did remain in the service of The Salvation Army, he or she was bound to the conditions of that service. "The first condition of that service is implicit, unquestioning obedience. The Salvationist is taught to obey as is the soldier on the field of battle."[9]

Finally, it should be noted that there were many people loyal to Booth who shared his sympathies, both his theological sympathies and his organizational ones. They did so because they shared much of the institutional power with him, and they wanted both to support the structure of The Salvation Army and provide goals and direction for the movement.

In this regard, the two most important family members were Catherine Mumford Booth, his wife, and Bramwell Booth, the eldest son and the successor to William Booth as the second General of The Salvation Army. Catherine Booth was a moving force as The Salvation Army developed such doctrines as personal holiness and the role of women in ministry. Bramwell Booth, William Booth's Chief of the Staff (second in command of The Salvation Army), was interested in the doctrines of personal and institutional holiness, and played a vital role in the formation of the organizational structure of The Salvation Army.

A third person, George Scott Railton, also participated in the institutional power with the Booths until the early 1890s. An ascetic and disciplined person by nature, he also espoused especially Booth's understanding of the doctrine of holiness, and helped to shape the initial organizational structure of The Salvation Army. He was the first to hold the highest rank, that of commissioner, of The Salvation Army. In 1880 William Booth stated: "Next to the influence of my own family upon this movement, no influence has been greater than that of George Scott Railton."[10]

Once The Salvation Army was established, its faith and practice were set forth in *The Doctrines and Disciplines of The Salvation Army*. Benjamin Field had published a work on Christian theology, and "there can be no question that the basic source for Booth's *Doctrines and Disciplines* was the Rev. Benjamin Field's *The Student's Handbook of Christian Theology*, originally published in 1868."[11] Field's work was considerably longer and more detailed than Booth's *Doctrines and Disciplines*, but Booth selected those doctrines which were pertinent to his own thinking at the time and central to the work of The Salvation Army.[12]

The Development of The Salvation Army After 1878

The development of The Salvation Army after 1878 is best understood by explaining the increasing public acceptance of a developing movement and by acknowledging the growth of the movement.

Evidence of the public recognition began between 1882 and 1883 when the Anglican Church, under the leadership of Archbishop Tait, initiated negotiations with The Salvation Army as to whether the Army would become part of the Church of England. However, The Salvation Army was now nearly twenty years old, and had therefore established itself as an independent movement. Such characteristics as its authoritarian structure, its rather free-and-easy approach to religious meetings, its evolving into a non-practicing understanding of the sacraments, and its insistence on women participating equally with men in the ministry prevented it from being absorbed into the Church of England.

Added to this was a gradual recognition of the work of the Army by the British monarchy. The clearest evidence of this is the correspondence between William and Catherine Booth and Queen Victoria in the mid 1880s. By 1897, the Queen was referring to Booth as General. Booth sent a message to Queen Victoria in connection with her Diamond Jubilee, and the Queen's reply from Windsor Castle was addressed to General Booth.

Arch Wiggins in volume four of *The History of The Salvation Army* wrote that "It was noted with considerable satisfaction that Her Majesty had graciously and specifically acknowledged the General's well-won right to his title, so bringing to an end the small-minded prejudice which from time to time had denied this to him."[13] The culmination of royal acceptance, however, came on June 24, 1904 when Booth was received at Buckingham Palace by King Edward VII.

Consideration of the growth of The Salvation Army is also important in order to understand the development of the Army after 1878. After 1878 The Salvation Army grew rapidly, not only in England but in other parts of the world, including America.[14] Roland Robertson, commenting on the growth of The Salvation Army in England from 1878 to 1881 in his article entitled "The Salvation Army: the Persistence of Sectarianism," wrote:

> The fact that The Salvation Army came to figure so prominently in the religious life of England, in effect within the space of three years, is on all accounts a noteworthy phenomenon. In some towns it ranked very high in the order of bodies contributing to the total attendances. For example, in Runcorn it was first with 2,759 out of 9,447, and in Barrow, Barnsley, Bristol, Hull, Mexborough, Scarborough, Worksop, Wrexham and Cheltenham it was either second or third. In terms of absolute attendance, the greatest strength of the Army was in Hull (11,394), Bristol (11,035), Nottingham (4,245), Bradford (4,206), Sheffield (4,115), Portsmouth (3,900), Scarborough (3,380), and Barrow (3,088).[15]

Charles Booth in Volume I of *Life and Labour of the People in London* wrote that "The Salvation Army, originated in the East of London in 1865, claims (Christmas 1888) to have 7107 officers, 2587 corps, and 653 outposts, established in 33 countries or colonies; and so rapid is its growth, that 1423 officers and 325 corps have been added in the past 12 months."[16] Charles Booth's own observation about the overall work of The Salvation Army was that "So far the Army occupies a very strong position."[17]

Needless to say, such growth was important to the continued development of The Salvation Army after 1878. It was also the most important source of confirmation to Booth of the validity of the continued existence of his Army. He was consistently persuaded that "God has decreed to deliver the world by God and man combined. And therefore that [sic] the more God manifests Himself, and the more men that respond to that manifestation, the easier it is for the exercise of faith. A worldwide Army means a mighty increase of confidence for the subjugation of the world."[18]

The Theology of William Booth

The Doctrine of Revelation

This chapter begins, as Chapter I began, with Booth's theology of revelation. In his later years, he was still a Biblicist and found in the Bible the necessary support for what he believed to be theologically significant. However, while the Bible functioned earlier as a text for revivalist preaching, it functioned later in another way—yet not a way which supplanted the first, for Booth continued his public preaching until his death in 1912. However, as he shifted away from the institutional Church and away from the authority of that Church toward his own institution, he had to find a new source of authority for the direction that he was taking. That new source was the Bible. By finding military imagery in the Bible, and sometimes by imposing military imagery upon the Bible, William Booth legitimated the military nature of his movement as one expression of the Body of Christ. The Salvation Army did not always have the blessing of the institutional church, but, Booth believed, it did have the blessing of a higher authority—Scripture—and therefore of the God of Scripture.

He constantly related the imagery of the Bible to The Salvation Army at this later stage of his theology. In his work entitled *Religion for Every Day*, he referred to "Salvationists in Ephesus"[19] while writing about a passage from the book of Ephesians. In discussing a passage from II Kings, he stated:

> There is a chapter in Church history which you can look up. You will find it in 2 Kings xxiii and 3, where The

> Salvation Army of that day came forth and made a treaty
> with God, and to their everlasting credit were true to it,
> for it is said of them, 'They stood to their covenant.'[20]

He saw in the Bible the confirmation and legitimacy that he sought for the work of The Salvation Army. As will be noted later in this chapter, he developed a particular view of the nature of the work of The Salvation Army, and the Bible served as an important source of this revelation. "We have to serve God and save the world—or, as large a portion of it as we possibly can. That is settled. It has been revealed to us; written down for us in the Bible, and written in our hearts by the Holy Ghost."[21] He became convinced that the Bible had revealed to him that the highest service he could render to people on this earth was to rescue them "from this position of antagonism to the Divine Government."[22]

Experience continued to be an invaluable confirmation of revelation in the later life and ministry of Booth. "Whatever other people say about me," he wrote, "I know full well that the General is nothing if not practical."[23] He often prided himself on being "an out-and-out utilitarian."[24] He was not a mystic or a visionary in the sense that he was unaware of what was going on around him and of how his personal experiences had an impact upon him. He was a person whose experiences and empirical observations were important in his theology. Nowhere would this become more evident in his later theology than in his understanding of redemption.

There were two characteristics of the man that, although present in his earlier ministry, were intensified as he grew older. Both of these characteristics were forged through personal experience and therefore deserve mention here. The first was that Victorian optimism mentioned in Chapter I. With Booth's growing movement developed his own expanding optimism about the possibilities of that Army to effect both spiritual and social change. "Just as political expansion helped British self-confidence, so missionary expansion helped Christian self-confidence."[25] Booth's Wesleyan doctrine of unlimited atonement also shaped his optimism about the future.

The second characteristic was his toleration. Because his own Army became well established, and because his undivided attention to that Army became critical, he was not a person given to judging the rest of the Church. When speaking of the Church or of other denominations or of particular men or women, his language was usually amiable and often praiseworthy.

Nevertheless, he became increasingly convinced of the divine origin of The Christian Mission and The Salvation Army, and the responsibility of people in those groups was to be faithful to the work God had given them without being critical or judgmental of what other people were or were not doing. "My comrades," he characteristically said, "never mind other people. Take your eyes off them. What do we accomplish?"[26] In an overview of his work to date in July, 1894, Booth stated:

> My natural yearning for success is, perhaps, almost a weakness; together with my impatience as to the feeble progress that the Kingdom of Heaven makes in its extension in the world, notwithstanding the efforts put forth, compels me to be not only willing but delighted to discover any improved plan for accelerating the pace. I readily recognize the mosaic character of these influences. While teaching others, others have taught me.[27]

The Doctrine of God the Father

As has been pointed out in the previous chapter, Booth's primary concentration was not on God the Father. This was true in his earlier theology, and it was still the case in his later theology. Once the doctrine of God the Father had been formulated in The Christian Mission and established as a doctrine of The Salvation Army by the Deed Poll of 1878, Booth's primary concern with the doctrine of God the Father was in connection with his work—he constantly affirmed the divine origin of The Salvation Army. It was of God.

This affirmation became increasingly important for Booth. Without that all would be lost. Without that, Booth would feel himself engaged in a purely human endeavor. He could not have that. Such affirmation will become evident in this chapter in the section which deals with the doctrine of the Church in the later theology of Booth.

The Doctrine of God the Son

Booth's doctrine of Christ took on a new dimension in his later theology. Here, there was an emphasis on incarnation, in keeping with the prevailing theology of the nineteenth century. Jesus Christ became the great model to be followed. This imagery of Christ served two purposes for Booth: Christ became the model leader to be followed into universal redemption, and Christ, as the spiritual leader or spiritual General of The Salvation Army, certainly provided legitimacy for the Army's existence.

Combining the imagery of Jesus as model with military imagery became common for Booth in his later theology, especially after The Salvation Army was well established, and Booth continued to employ such imagery well after this second stage in his theology. This imagery comes to the fore first in *The War Cry* of February 21, 1885, in which he wrote an article about the work of Jesus Christ entitled "The Model Salvation Soldier."[28] In other articles, he referred to Jesus as the General,[29] or as a brave warrior.[30] In his book entitled *The General's Letters, 1885,* William Booth wrote:

> I said last week, that after all our Model Warrior was
> the Lord Jesus. His life and teaching, taken together,
> constitute the pattern and teach the only true method
> in which our campaign for the deliverance of man from
> sin and devils is to be carried on. This was declared
> by Peter, a celebrated General, who fought gloriously

in the early history of this War, when he said, "Even hereunto were ye called"—that is, enlisted—"because Christ also suffered for you, leaving an example that you should follow in his steps." If the Holy Ghost commanded the early Salvationists to fight after the pattern of their Master, surely the same obligation is binding upon US.[31]

For William Booth, "Jesus Christ is the heart of the Christian Religion."[32] While reflecting upon his work in January, 1889, he wrote that "the very first article in my creed, which I held with all the certainty of a direct revelation from heaven, was a belief in the sacrificing love of Christ to men, love which impelled Him continually to seek their welfare."[33] However, he continued to raise the image of this "Salvationist's example,"[34] this "pattern man,"[35] after 1889 to a higher level when he stated that Jesus Christ was not only the model of humanity after which characters will be formed and shaped, but He was also the model of divinity for people. In his article entitled "The Christ-Man," he wrote:

> To have the Christianity of Christ is in the first place to have the nature of Christ—the Divine nature .... If you are to be a Divine man you must have the Divine nature—you must be born again, not of the flesh, not of opinions, not of creeds, but you must be born of the Spirit—made into a new creature—a new man in Christ Jesus; and nothing can be put in the place of this.[36]

When William Booth stated "Let us enquire Behold the Man! We have agreed that He is our Model,"[37] it is understood that he had a high view of the Person and work of Jesus Christ for those who by faith saw this Christ as their pattern for both their human natures and their conformity to the image of Christ.

Booth still held to the uniqueness of Jesus Christ as only Lord and Savior, or, as Salvation Army doctrine affirmed, "truly God and truly man." He did not argue the point about the possibility of a divine nature of some sort in human beings. He believed it was possible. But he never affirmed a nature which would make people equal with Jesus Christ. Nevertheless, did Booth believe that people could be as they were intended to be before the fall? Did he believe that the *imago dei*, restored after justification, insured a divine nature in people? Or was he trying to understand the implications of what it means for the believer to conform to the image of God in the sense described, for example, in Colossians 3:10?

He did not address these questions or controversies. In any case, depending on the context, it appears that his language about the divine nature in people was synonymous, in his own mind at least, with justification and perhaps even sometimes with sanctification. It was, however, a strange way of describing either of those doctrines.

However, once this imagery of Jesus as model was well established, it was next important that people tie into this imagery. It was critical that people see their lives as inextricably bound with this Christ, especially with the Christ whom Booth identified with his Salvation Army by using the military language for Christ that became so familiar to the followers of William Booth.

Just as there was no Christianity without Christ, so it was equally true that "There is no Christ without Christianity. No man has any right to conclude that he has any saving interest in Christ who does not realise in his own soul the reconciliation and peace and love that Christ proclaimed and died to obtain, and who is not at the same time endeavoring to spread these blessings abroad. You can't have Christ without being a Christ-man—a Christian."[38]

For Booth, the most natural way of identification of the believer with Christ was identification with Him in His sufferings, a theme common to Booth. It was the identification of the believer with the cross of Christ that was essential. Therefore, following Christ meant self-denial, surrender, toil, and suffering. Following Christ meant that the life of the Salvationist would be a difficult one. Such identification, therefore, served at least four functions in the theology of William Booth. First, it gave legitimacy to the strenuous work to which Booth called his followers. Second, it was a witness to the world that the believer was on the side of the atoning Christ and not on the side of the world and the devil. Third, it was ultimately the means of the redemption of the world, which was the primary function of the Church in Booth's understanding of the Church at this stage in his theology, which will be considered in this chapter. "If you go you will have to suffer; there is no other way of going .... If he suffers for Christ he saves, and if he saves he suffers."[39] Finally, suffering was a means of perfecting the person, which in turn was necessary if the above three functions were ever to be realized. In an article entitled "The Imitation of Jesus Christ" written for *The War Cry* in 1893, Booth asked:

> But why the Cross? There is no other way by which God can create that perfection of character which He wants in His people than by the Cross. Luxury, ease, prosperity weaken and deteriorate human nature. Hardship, sorrow, loss, persecution and scorn; in other words, the Cross, raises, improves, refines and sanctifies. It is by suffering we are made perfect. Not that there is any power in suffering, taken alone, to purify, expand and ennoble the soul; but suffering drives us to God, and it is God that saves.[40]

The Doctrine of God the Holy Spirit

William Booth's understanding of the Person of the Holy Spirit did not undergo the kind of change evidenced in his doctrine of Christ. Booth's conception of the Person of the Holy Spirit remained constant, and he identified that Person of the Trinity by the work which was done in the life of the believer and in the work of the Army.

The clear change was in Booth's understanding of the work of the Holy Spirit. That basic work was still one of sanctification, but sanctification of what? In this later stage of Booth's theology, he still affirmed the sanctification of the individual believer by faith, but he also affirmed the sanctification of his Army—institutional sanctification. With the development of his Army came a broader view of sanctification. Added to this corporate concept of sanctification was Booth's vision of the final direction, the eschatological goal, of sanctification—that is, the final conquest of the world, and the conquering of evil. Only a holy person could do a holy act. Likewise, only a people sanctified by the Holy Spirit could accomplish God's holy purpose of ultimate victory. In Booth's understanding of institutional sanctification, his Army was so sanctified. The sanctifying work of the Holy Spirit was still critical to Booth.

The Doctrine of the Fall

In his doctrine of the fall can be found another important change in the theology of William Booth. As has been noted, in the period of his ministry characterized by evangelistic preaching, his understanding of the fall was limited primarily to personal categories—sin and guilt. However, while those categories are still found in the preaching and writing of Booth in this second stage, they were matched by corporate categories—evil, total rebellion against God on a universal scale, and, consequently, alienation from God that led to a disordering of human society.

Booth and his Salvationists were now coming into conflict with evil in other forms than that of the lonely poor sinner on Whitechapel Road who was drawn to the revival meetings in a tent pitched in a Quaker burial ground. The Army now encountered opposition and even oppression from such opposite quarters as people of the Church who thought the Army to be a scandal, to tavern owners who were opposed to the Army's insistence on total abstinence. Physical violence ensued, and Salvationists began to die in their street meetings. "But the Salvationists excited a deadlier enmity by their fierce antipathy to drink. The rage of the brewers and the publicans and the drunkards was leagued against them, and it received the startling support of the magistrates and the police."[41]

As the Army moved out of London into the larger world it began to realize the systemic nature of evil manifested in such forms as the vicious white slave trade of England. The involvement of Catherine Booth, Bramwell Booth, and W. T. Stead in the Purity Crusade to expose child prostitution in England and have the age of consent raised from thirteen brought this evil into clear focus to people of the Army, to the larger society, and to the consciousness of William Booth.

Other evils that the Army began to encounter included the oppressive poverty of industrial workers, the unsafe and unsanitary working and living conditions of the poor, and the indifference of legislators to reformation. These scandals were not only England's however. The Army began to understand that they were universal.

In attempting to articulate the nature of such total spiritual evil, Booth commonly personified that evil either in the form of Satan or the devil, or in the form of the world, which he perceived as fallen but not beyond redemption. Thus, in the later Booth, evil, Satan, and the world became synonymous terms, used interchangeably in his writing and preaching. Examples of his use of these corporate images of evil can be found pervading his later theology. For example, in 1885 he asked, "When will those who make a loud profession of their desire that Christ should have all the world for His inheritance, and the uttermost parts of the earth for His possession, recognize the patent fact that those who possess it will not give it up without a struggle."[42]

Once this imagery became common in this second stage of his theology, Booth continued to use such imagery for the rest of his ministry. In 1892 he wrote that "the world and the devil and his creatures—and he has plenty of creatures to help him—are still engaged day and night, endeavoring to quench this Pentecostal Fire, and would do so with marvellous rapidity but for the oil of grace with which the Spirit of the living God fans and feeds the flames."[43] In one of the last articles prepared for *The War Cry* Booth wrote the following:

> The world, this very world, including this very England,
> which never ceases boasting of its freedom, is sold
> under sin, held in slavery by Satan, who has usurped
> the place and power and revenues of Jehovah, and who
> is indeed its lord and master, and to deliver it and to
> fulfill to the very letter of the Master's command an
> army of deliverance, of redemption, of emancipation
> is wanted.[44]

These images, however, were spiritual images of forces which were at war for the souls of men and women on a universal scale. The next chapter will take note of the most important change in the later theology of William Booth, a change that included social as well as spiritual redemption as a means of understanding all the dimensions of salvation. It is interesting to note that Booth's corporate imagery of evil also changed to include social as well as spiritual categories.

Booth's article in 1889 in *All The World* in which he first articulated his changed theology of redemption is also significant for its expression of an expanded conceptualization of corporate and institutional evil. His language of evil broadened to reflect and to accommodate his changed theology, and he wrote, for example, of "unjust laws that seemed to favor the perpetuation of the calamitous circumstances that pressed so heavily on the wretched multitudes,"[45] and of the outward hell of "poverty, drunkenness, debauchery, crime, slavery, war and every other form of outward misery."[46]

Before leaving this discussion of Booth's concept of evil in this second stage of his theology, it is important to note that his theology of evil at this point ultimately strengthened rather than weakened his theology of redemption. He did not believe in an open dualism of some sort. Evil was not ultimate or permanent. While recognizing the power of evil, this kind of affirmation was common for Booth: "I tell you you will win the race yet. The devil says you won't, but he is a liar, you are going to win."[47] In an article appropriately entitled "Fight!" which he wrote for *All The World* in May, 1885, he stated:

> What are you to fight? Evil in every form. War to the knife with sin! Vulgar or respectable, clothed in broadcloth or satin, or veiled in filthy rags, wherever you find it, plunge your sword into it. Call it by its right name. Hate it. Loathe it. Uncover it and make men hate it and put it from them in disgust.[48]

And after his theology evolved to include a broader concept of salvation, he still believed in the ultimate conquest of evil, even of social and institutional evil. He wrote:

> I saw that when the Bible said, "He that believeth shall be saved," it meant not only saved from the miseries of the future world, but from the miseries of this also. That it came with the promise of salvation here and now: from hell and sin and vice and crime and idleness and extravagance, and consequently very largely from poverty and disease, and the majority of kindred woes.[49]

The Doctrine of the Church

It is unfortunate that even in the later stages of his theology Booth referred to the Church without defining it precisely. That problem was encountered in the last chapter. However, we take it from his writings that the Church was primarily those believers who were justified by faith and bore witness to that by word and deed. Any understanding of the Church for Booth in every stage of his theology included the concept of mission.

Booth did develop an ecclesiology once The Christian Mission was established and once the work of The Christian Mission was formulated in 1870. That ecclesiology was based on the simple

47

mission of preaching the Gospel and saving souls. Here was a group with a mission.

However, as the next chapter will demonstrate, once The Salvation Army was established, the group added a mission. After 1889 Booth's doctrine of the Church was stated in such a way that it accommodated his changed theology—the group now had a mission to preach the Gospel and save souls and to redeem society.

The Church became for Booth the agent of redemption from evil, and in his later theology his doctrine of the Church became more and more clearly focused as it related to its redemptive missions. His doctrine of the Church at this second stage of his ministry and theology served to legitimate his Army, which in turn legitimated the redemptive work which sustained that Army.

William Booth was concerned for the preservation of The Salvation Army. Therefore, he was sustained by his belief that The Salvation Army was divinely ordained, and that it was a renewal in the nineteenth century and twentieth century of the Church in the New Testament, the early Church, the Reformation Church, and the Wesleyan revival. He was convinced that The Christian Mission and The Salvation Army were manifestations of the historic Church from its inception in the New Testament and were an integral part of that Church on earth.

This being the case, Booth called upon his officers and soldiers at this second stage of his theology to "make another chapter of the Acts of the Apostles, by being an Apostle yourself."[50] Such a theme continued even after this second stage in Booth's theology, and he later wrote that "as truly as He originated the Great Church at Jerusalem, so surely has He, by His wonderful power, made this Salvation Army."[51] "I say with Peter," he wrote in 1889, "'Look not on me, as though by my own power or holiness I have done these things. The God of Abraham and of Isaac and of Jacob—the God of our Fathers has glorified His Son Jesus Christ' in this fragment of my history."[52]

These emphases are further evident in a long address delivered to Salvationists at Exeter Hall in 1886. Part of that address is worth quoting for two reasons: it best articulates Booth's understanding of The Salvation Army as a biblical movement that manifested itself in the nineteenth century, and it exemplifies the limits of Booth's understanding of incarnation—Christ came in the flesh in that part of the body known as The Salvation Army. At that address Booth stated the following:

> If I did not think that the Lord was in this movement I would have nothing more to do with it, and much less would I ask you to carry it on. I believe that The Salvation Army is as much of God as Israel was of God. I do not say—far be it from me—that there are not other Israels and Jacobs, but they had got [sic] generals who can speak for them. I have confidence to speak, however, for The Salvation Army. I believe Jesus Christ has come over again in this movement, and that not only in the Spirit, but in the manner of His coming. There has been a remarkable resemblance to His coming 1800 years ago, when He came in poverty in Bethlehem.
>
> Twenty-one years ago this Army was started; we celebrated our majority at this Congress. Twenty-one years ago we may say that Christ came again in poverty in an old tent in a burial ground in Whitechapel. When he came 1800 years ago His disciples were poor, despised working men. The world hated Him in this. The Pharisees, Sadducees, and the Scribes were against Him then, and many clergymen and infidels, and many church and chapel people are against Him now—at least they are against this form of His coming. They did not see Him then, and they do not understand Him now. And so you might run through His history and ours, and you will find I am certain a very remarkable resemblance to the coming of the Lord Jesus Christ 1800 years ago and the coming of the Lord Jesus Christ

in this marvelous manifestation of The Salvation Army
today. I believe this movement is of God; I am sure it
is; I know it is; I feel it is.[53]

In this regard, it is significant that William Booth considered
himself and his movement to be part of the universal Church, an
important part of the body of Christ here on earth. "It was William
Booth's earnest and oft-stated determination that he would be no
party to the creation of a new sect."[54] He feared a sectarian spirit
arising within The Salvation Army, by which he meant a kind of
world-denying and church-condemning spirit. He wanted to avoid
these postures. In an article entitled "What is The Salvation Army?"
written in 1882, he asked, "What will it grow to? Who can guess? I
cannot. Never, I hope, into a sect. We have taken and shall continue
to take every precaution against this. Warned by the failure of John
Wesley in maintaining his unsectarian position, we are trying to
avoid what we think were his mistakes."[55] As part of his precaution
to avoid a sectarian spirit, he strove to maintain friendly relations
with churches, to gain sympathies from godly people, and to spread
"a spirit of love and hearty cooperation that will do much to lessen
the dividing walls of sectarianism."[56]

For William Booth, especially in his later theology, the one true
sign of the Church was participation in the work of redemption,
both personal redemption and, after 1889, social redemption, leading ultimately to the final establishment of the Kingdom of God.
This work was fundamentally connected to Booth's doctrine of
holiness, because he believed that only a holy people could accomplish a holy work and achieve a holy goal.

Therefore, his theology eventually included a non-practicing
position regarding the sacraments. His reasons for arriving at this
position are complex and debatable, but Roland Robertson in his
article entitled "The Salvation Army: The Persistence of Sectarianism" is incorrect when he attributes this part of Booth's theology
to institutional calculation alone. Booth's non-practicing position
was not, as Robertson affirms, a result of his desire to maintain

the hierarchical organization and prevent sacramental power from falling into the hands and under the control of lesser officers in the organizational hierarchy. Robertson writes that a denial of the place of the sacraments in the life of the Army was connected with the hierarchical structure of the Army, "for with so much power wielded by the officers, the temptations to interpose the latter as mediators between God and the Salvation soldier were very strong."[57] Such an assumption is wrong for two reasons. First, it advances a high view of the sacraments and of sacramental power, a view which Booth never espoused. Second, it reduces Booth's theological decisions solely to organizational concerns, and that leads to a myopic view of Booth and his theology.

Robertson also incorrectly assumes that Booth's view of the sacraments constituted a kind of anti-sacramentalism. This is untrue. Booth was non-practicing in his later theology, but he was never anti-sacramental. He held that participation in the work of redemption was the one indispensable sign of the true Church, and therefore did not view the sacraments as concomitant indispensable signs. But his non-practicing position was rooted also in his view of Christian holiness. As William Booth clarified his doctrine of holiness—both personal and institutional—he drew the implication that all of life was to be holy for the believer and for the Church. For example, he wrote that "nothing should be allowed in conversation that is contrary to sound doctrine."[58] Thus the life of the individual and the life of the Church were sacred. Because of this, external ordinances of any kind were unnecessary to demonstrate periodically that which should be demonstrated continually.

Therefore, for Booth, the external act of baptism was not what he believed either the Scripture or his experience dictated. He wrote:

> I cannot accept any obligation as binding upon my
> conscience, neither will I seek to bind any upon yours,
> to do, or believe, or teach anything for which authority

cannot be furnished from the Word of God, or which God Himself does not reveal to us by His Spirit, as our present duty.[59]

Rather, the baptism of the Holy Spirit was the emphasis of Scripture as Booth read it, and that baptism, rather than water baptism, became central to Booth's theology. One author has rightly noted:

> Baptism, therefore, was for William Booth a detail of symbolism, and he left it freely to his followers to decide whether they would be baptised or not: he felt no vital concern in the matter. His emphasis was on conversion, the conversion of the adult and intelligent individual, and this was the first and greatest of his preachings. But beyond the arrest of the sinner, and the awakening of the soul to the living fact of the Living God, lay the path of Holiness; and here William Booth could not stop and leave conversion to follow its own evolution.[60]

Likewise, the external act of communion was not what he believed either the Scriptures or his own experience emphasized. Booth implied from his doctrine of holiness that not one act of communion once a week or once a month was what was of importance. Rather, all of life was holy, all of life was sacramental—that is, Booth said, "every meal of which we partake should be a Sacrament, and every action we perform a part of our Religion."[61] He explained this concept in further detail in the following way:

> That is what the Apostle Paul meant when he said, "Whether therefore ye eat, or drink, or whatsoever ye do, do all to the glory of God." Now if this command of the Holy Spirit, given by Paul, is observed, you will see that every meal we partake of will become a sacrament, and every duty we perform will be an act of religion, and every day we live will be a sacred day, a Sabbath of peace and joy in the Holy Ghost.[62]

The Doctrine of Sanctification

All of this leads to the observation that a fundamental aspect of Booth's doctrine of redemption in his later theology was that of sanctification. He still embraced the doctrine of sanctification by faith for the believer in his later theology. In fact, his best work on this doctrine, a book entitled *Purity of Heart*, was written in 1902. Sanctification by faith was still important. It was the ultimate answer to the problem of personal sin and guilt. The basic tenets of the doctrine were still taught and preached: it was a second definite work of God's grace in the heart of the believer; it was appropriated by faith; it was for all believers; and believers could be assured that they were sanctified.[63]

However, in his later theology William Booth began to understand the doctrine of sanctification in corporate categories and images as well as personal ones. It becomes clear in his later theology exactly why he interpreted sanctification in this wider dimension. First, sanctification was a final answer to the problem of evil. By allying sanctification with the ultimate conquest of the world and of evil, Booth destroyed any concept of the finality of evil.

Second, his doctrine of sanctification gave legitimacy to his organization. He became convinced that God not only sanctifies individuals, but He also sanctifies groups. The doctrine of sanctification took on a new dimension for Booth as his Army grew and developed. Corporate sanctification, or institutional sanctification, became an important sign that The Salvation Army was of divine, and not merely human, origin. This continued to characterize his later theology. In a *War Cry* article in 1892 the Founder exhorted his readers in this way: "Cast yourselves on God. Keep on watching and praying and believing and expecting for me, for yourselves, for the whole Army at home and abroad, for the mighty baptism of burning fire!"[64] He reiterated this in 1909:

The Salvation Army has known a great deal of this
Divine inspiration. It is itself the creation of the Holy
Spirit. All it knows of life and vitality, and all the power
it possesses to bless the world, come from the Holy
Spirit; and to this day waves of Divine influence, in a
lesser or greater measure, are sweeping over it which
proceed from Him alone.[65]

Third, Booth's wider understanding of sanctification became
fundamental because this work of God in believers and in the
Church was a preparation for the final redemptive purpose of
God—the establishment of the Kingdom of God. This aspect of
sanctification prevented Booth's concept of holiness from being
monastic—it was not a doctrine that called for separation from
the evil world until the work of redemption was completed by
God Himself alone.

At this stage in Booth's theology, there was a natural transition
from the doctrine of sanctification as a means of preparation for
redemption, and the doctrine of the Kingdom of God as a result
of the work of redemption by God's holy people here on earth.
In short, the doctrines of sanctification and the Kingdom of God
became so inextricably linked to one another at this stage that it
would be impossible to consider one doctrine without considering
the other. They cannot be treated separately. "If you are a holy man
or woman you will help forward the War, and spread the glory
of Christ's Name far more effectively than you will if you are not
fully saved. Holy people are the great need of the world. I am sure
they are one of the great wants of the Army."[66] Not surprisingly,
those who shared the organizational and institutional power with
William Booth espoused this same theology which gave legitimacy
to the organization. They, too, were convinced of these doctrinal
principles: the nature of institutional holiness, and the ultimate
redemptive purposes of that holiness—the conquest of the world.[67]

The Doctrine of the Kingdom of God and the Millennium

The culmination of Booth's theology of redemption in these later years came in his understanding of the Kingdom of God. This eschatological strain in his theology became necessary for the two reasons which prevailed in those later years: the establishment of the Kingdom of God on earth was the final answer to evil, the final triumph over evil; and, its establishment legitimated the very existence of The Salvation Army, which Booth was increasingly certain had been chosen by God as the chief instrument to bring about that Kingdom and provided a vision of hope for his movement.

William Booth believed in redemption. In his earlier years, he stressed redemption of the individual by justification by faith in Jesus Christ and by sanctification by faith through the work of the Holy Spirit. In his later years, he expanded his vision of redemption—he believed in the redemption of the world by the overthrow of the forces in the world that were in rebellion against God, and by the setting up of the Kingdom of God here on earth. This was done as a cooperative venture between God and His people.

He used the language common to his day when he spoke of the Kingdom of God on earth. He envisioned the establishment of the millennium. Millennial themes had been the subject of countless books, articles, discussions, and movements from the period of the New Testament to the nineteenth century. Neither Booth's concepts nor his practical applications of those concepts were new. However, his distinctive contribution and focus was in the relationship of his Army and his theology to the establishment of the millennium. The fundamental wing of the Protestant world of the nineteenth century was engaged in millennial thinking, and one of the finest books on this subject is Ernest R. Sandeen's work entitled *The Roots of Fundamentalism*.[68] But, while Sandeen deals with millennialism within fundamental Protestantism quite extensively, he emphasizes premillennial thinking, which is primarily the belief that the gospel was not intended nor was it going to accomplish the salvation of the world, but that, instead, the world was growing increasingly corrupt and rushing toward imminent judgment; the belief that Christ would literally return to this earth and the Jews be restored to Palestine before the commencement of that millennial age; and the belief that this whole panorama of coming glory and judgment was explicitly foretold in the prophecies where one could, if taught by the Spirit, discover the truth and be ready for the coming of the bridegroom.[69]

Sandeen does not treat with equal force another millennial view which was prominent in the nineteenth century and the beginning of the twentieth century. That other millennial view, known as postmillenialism, was considered a viable option by William Booth. He was a postmillennialist. Briefly, postmillennialism "holds that the millennium will come first, usually 'as the fruit of the present Christian agencies now at work in the world,' and that the Second Coming or the delivering agency will occur at the end of the process."[70] A clearer and more succinct definition of postmillennialism is found in an excellent work by Donald W. Dayton entitled *Discovering an Evangelical Heritage*. Postmillennialism is the expectation of "Christ to return in judgment after a millennial reign of one thousand years."[71] Dayton correctly goes on to affirm that "reform activity was in part to prepare the way for the millennium, which was in turn a reflection of the vision of the 'state of the perfect society' that drew Evangelicals into reform."[72]

Booth's millennial thinking became part of the fabric of the theology of The Salvation Army in his day. In this regard, his millennialism, in the context of his total theological system, in the context of The Salvation Army and its ministry and social concern, and in the context of other millennial dreams, was not odd, was not strange, and was not insignificantly visionary. Rather, it provided both justification for the existence of The Salvation Army as well as hope for the primary work of The Salvation Army, and was consistently part of millennial thinking which prevailed in The Salvation Army at that time. It is highly important that this be understood in order to explain this aspect of the theology of William Booth.

He was convinced that this work of redemption was the will of God. He reasoned analogously: just as God willed that an individual be saved, so God extended that will to the whole world, and He wanted the entire world to be saved. "We must increase the speed if we are to keep pace with the yearnings of the Almighty Heart of Love that would have all men to be saved."[73] Given that fact, he was equally convinced that God's people on earth were the agencies of that redemption, and none were better suited or qualified for that than Salvationists.[74]

Here William Booth's single-mindedness and his inextricable relationship with The Salvation Army came to his service.[75] He became increasingly convinced that he and his people were to have a significant part to play in the establishment of such a Kingdom. It must be remembered that setting some sort of time frame for the establishment of the Kingdom of God by reading the nineteenth and twentieth centuries back into the books of Daniel and Revelation was of no interest to Booth. He was concerned, however, that his people understand their place in the process of redemption, and that they be properly motivated, realizing all along that there was a divine organizational goal toward which they were marching—the Kingdom of God. It was that goal which gave the work such significance in the lives of his followers. "When God's people wake up to the importance of this great War, and go forth to engage in it after this fashion, the millennium will not be very far away."[76] On that practical, pastoral level rested a chief concern of William Booth. On May 30, 1885 he wrote:

> I want to see a new translation of the Bible into the hearts and conduct of living men and women. I want an improved translation—or transference it might be called—of the commandments and promises and

teachings and influences of this Book to the minds
and feelings and words and activities of the men and
women who hold onto it and swear by it and declare
it to be an inspired Book and the only authorized rule
of life .... It is of no use making correct translations
of words if we cannot get the words translated into
life . ... Wayfaring men, though fools, can make this
translation, and fifteen years' perseverance in it will, I
have not the shadow of a doubt, go a long way towards
bringing in the millennium.[77]

That kind of hopeful relationship of The Salvation Army and
the establishment of the Kingdom of God continued to prevail
in Booth's thinking throughout the rest of his life. His enduring
postmillennial vision continued unabated, and The Salvation Army
continued to be for Booth the agency best suited for the work of
universal redemption. In "What is The Salvation Army?" he wrote
the following:

If it be wise and lawful and desirable for men to be
banded together and organized after the best method
possible to liberate an enslaved nation, establish it in
liberty, and overcome its foes, then surely it must be
wise and lawful and desirable for the people of God to
join themselves together after the fashion most effective
and forcibly to liberate a captive world, and to overcome the enemies of God and man.[78]

He best summarized his word to The Salvation Army concerning the universal work of redemption and the part played in that
work by The Salvation Army in his letter to his officers around the
world in 1909 entitled *To My Officers: A Letter From The General
on His Eightieth Birthday*. There he wrote the following:

I want you to stand up more boldly and firmly than
you ever have done for the great object for which God

has made you Salvation Army Officers ... it consists in any intelligent, practical partnership with God in the great business of saving the world.

This you may take to be:
1. The putting down of the rebellion of man against the Divine government.
2. The expulsion of all wrongdoing from the earth.
3. The dethronement of the devils that now occupy the hearts of men.
4. The universal acceptance of men of Jesus Christ as their Sovereign Lord.
5. The bringing about of the reign of righteousness, and the obedience of the entire race to the law of love.

There can be no possible room for doubt in your minds, as to the object being the Divinely appointed end at which, as Salvation Army Officers, you are to aim.[79]

However, as desirous as he was for the establishment of the Kingdom of God and the setting up of the millennium, he held that the Kingdom of God was primarily a spiritual kingdom, and could not be ushered in and sustained by human effort apart from God. He knew that many people who made no claims to God or Christianity longed for some sort of millennium, and even tried to fulfill that longing. But such social, educational, or political endeavors apart from God were quite useless to Booth and to his theology.

He dealt with this issue in his later writing and preaching, partly because people from outside his own theological sensitivities were placing various millennial schemes before him. In the third article on "The Imitation of Jesus Christ" which he penned for *The War Cry* on October 7, 1893, he wrote clearly about this:

There is no Christianity without Christ. As you cannot have Christ without being a Christian, so you cannot

have the distinct blessings of Christianity without the
possession of that Christ who is the Author of it. Men
admire Christianity, go into raptures over it, chart its
praises, and admit its divinity and desirability. They
long after the reign of peace and purity in their own
hearts, and an era of goodwill and justice and love on
this poor distracted earth, when "The wolf shall dwell
with the lamb, and the leopard shall lie down with the
kid; and the calf and the young lion and the fatling
together; and a little child shall lead them." When there
shall be no more oppression and cruelty, or slavery, or
war; when men shall be kind and gentle and true to
each other; in short, when the spirit of heaven shall
reign upon the earth. But there is no way of getting at
this celestial condition of things but by the work of the
Holy Ghost received through Jesus Christ.

Men are trying hard to make a heaven without a
Saviour; to mend this Dilapidated Machine without
reference to the Divine Maker. Legislators, Press Men,
Humanitarians and Socialists, Poets and Painters, and
people of the imagination generally, are Labouring
night and day to discover and reach this promised land;
but they will find—indeed they do find—its attainment
without Jesus Christ to be impossible.

If it could be reached without Him, it seems to us
that the almighty Father made the most stupendous
mistake conceivable when He sacrificed His Son. If
Paradise—the Paradise lost—could be the Paradise
regained by Acts of Parliament, or Education, or
Scientific enquiries, or by Human Associations and
investigations of any descriptions whatever without the
aid of Jesus Christ, then why, oh why was he subjected
to all that agony? No! Neither the internal nor external
heaven can be won without Jesus Christ.[80]

Nowhere was it more important for Booth in his later theology to articulate his theological presuppositions of the Kingdom

of God, and the concomitant belief that human endeavors alone could not bring about the Kingdom of God on earth, than in his Darkest England Scheme and other endeavors of social salvation by the Army which will be treated in the following chapter. Booth stated that he was under no delusion "as to the possibility of inaugurating the Millennium by any social specific."[81]

He was, nevertheless, a practical man. He was not opposed to aid and assistance from secular sources for his program of physical and spiritual redemption. Those sources had to meet two criteria: they had to be in conformity with his theology. That is, they could not in any way be in direct opposition to God and orthodox Christianity. Second, they had to be practical. William Booth's doctrine of the Kingdom of God was not of some visionary, mystical existence that had no relationship to people's present life here on earth. He set forth those two criteria in *In Darkest England and the Way Out*. There he wrote:

> Of the schemes of those who propose to bring in a new heaven and a new earth by a more scientific distribution of the pieces of gold and silver in the trouser pockets of mankind, I need not say anything here. They may be good or they may not. I say nothing against any short cut to the Millennium that is compatible with the ten commandments. I intensely sympathise with the aspirations that lie behind all these Socialist dreams. But whether it is Henry George's Single Tax on Land Values, or Edward Bellamy's Nationalism, or the more elaborate schemes of the Collectivists, my attitude toward them all is the same. What these good people want to do, I also want to do. But I am a practical man, dealing with the actualities of today. I have no preconceived theories, and I flatter myself I am singularly free from prejudices. I am ready to sit at the feet of any who will show me any good. I keep my mind open on all these subjects: and I am quite prepared to hail with open arms any Utopia that is offered me. But

it must be within range of my finger-tips. It is of no
use to me if it is in the clouds. Cheques on the Bank of
Futurity I accept gladly enough as a free gift, but I can
hardly be expected to take them as if they were current
coin, or to try to cash them at the Bank of England.[82]

Booth was equally critical of religious people for offering little
hope for the Kingdom of God because of their theological presuppositions. They were as much deserving of criticism as those who
wished to bring about the millennium in some way apart from
Christianity. He wrote:

What are we to do with John Jones? That is the question. And to the solution of that question none of the
Utopias give me much help. For practical purposes
these dreamers fall under the condemnation they
lavish so freely upon the conventional religious people
who relieve themselves of all anxiety for the welfare
of the poor by saying that in the next world all will be
put right. This religious cant, which rids itself of all the
importunity of suffering humanity by drawing unne-
gotiable bills payable on the other side of the grave, is
not more impractical than the Socialist clap-trap which
postpones all redress of human suffering until after the
general overturn. Both take refuge in the Future to
escape a solution of the problem of the Present, and it
matters little to the sufferers whether the Future is on
this side of the grave or the other. Both are, for them,
equally out of reach.[83]

He was concerned to steer his theological course between two
dangers. On the one hand, he wished to stay clear of perceiving the
Kingdom of God in strictly spiritual, mystical, or utopian dimensions which had no relation to the actual lives of people in the
daily struggle for existence. On the other hand, he believed that the
Kingdom of God could be established only by religious means, and

he was aware of one of the potential dangers of his own theology if improperly understood by others—setting the social work of The Salvation Army loose from the theological moorings of that work, and eventually trusting in plans and programs which had no Christian foundation to accomplish the task of establishing the Kingdom of God.[84]

Because Booth's imagery of the millennium is important to his understanding of the goal of redemption in the Kingdom of God, it is necessary to give some attention to his conception of that millennium. As has been mentioned, he was a postmillennialist, but in this area, as in all other aspects of his theology, he perceived the first task of himself and The Salvation Army as that of working for the Kingdom of God, and neither arguing about points of theology nor telling people of other theological persuasions what they should believe.[85] He did inquire about any general concurrence of opinion that was prevalent in his day regarding the millennium, and some people, including those closest to him, were of the opinion that the millennium was coming soon. He referred to the millennium as "the good time coming,"[86] and he tried to discern the nature of the millennium from the Bible and from his own experience in order to inspire his officers and soldiers to fight a holy war of ultimate victory.

While not expending his energies trying scientifically or theologically to localize the millennium precisely either temporally or spatially, he did concern himself with identifying certain millennial distinctives so that his people would know the ultimate goal of their warfare. "I am not overly particular where I find the new heavens and the new earth," he wrote, "so that I do find them."[87] However, in his wisdom he did not include any millennial statement in the eleven doctrines of the Army. Indeed, some postmillennial doctrinal statement would have been difficult for the Army to defend as the twentieth century moved on after his death in 1912. He did expect that after the Kingdom of God was established, the millennium would have certain characteristics, and he also did expect that no lasting human blessedness would be possible without the presence of those characteristics.

Before dealing with them, however, there is a crucial link in the later theology of William Booth which must not be missed. As the previous quotations have shown, Booth made various references to the Kingdom of God earlier than 1889 and referred in a general way to the millennium as early as 1881. Nevertheless, just as his sensitivity toward the poor had been evident all his adult life but did not affect his theology until 1889-1890, so it was his theology of the Kingdom of God and the millennium: we find various references to these themes especially after the inauguration of The Salvation Army. However, they came into focus in 1890.

Indeed, the point needs to be made that Booth's expanded view of the Kingdom of God and the millennium coincides with his expanded view of salvation to include personal and social salvation, which will be treated in the next chapter. His clearest expression of the millennium was written in 1890 in an article entitled "The Millennium: or, the Ultimate Triumph of Salvation Army Principles." Two months after the writing of that article Booth published his *In Darkest England and The Way Out*, which was his clearest expression of his expanded theology of redemption.

And so, with the publication of "The Millennium," followed almost immediately by the publication of *In Darkest England and the Way Out*, the year 1890 proved to be one of the most significant years in the later theology of William Booth. The dual mission of The Salvation Army, undergirded by Booth's full understanding of redemption as both personal and social, was preparatory to the establishment of the millennial kingdom on earth. Likewise, Booth's increased emphasis on the possibility of a millennium provided a final eschatological vision for the conquest of God over the forces of evil as well as for the work of universal social redemption.

The first characteristic of the millennium was that God would be present among people, and that people would in turn acknowledge that presence. Booth taught that there was a natural set of consequential events in knowing God: all who know God will acknowledge His authority; all who acknowledge His authority will love and worship Him; and all who love and worship Him will delight to carry out His commandments and His will "as the angels do it in heaven."[88]

It was important to Booth that this acknowledgment of God be done openly and publicly in the context of a proper mixture of songs, prayers, worship, duty, and recreation. "God will be King, not only in theory, but in practice. He will not only reign, but govern. The will of God will be the law of earth, as it is the law of heaven."[89] Or, as Booth stated in a *War Cry* article in 1887, "Heaven and earth will come together, and Paradise will be here again."[90]

A second characteristic of the millennium was that of personal righteousness practiced by people in every aspect of life. In the millennium, people would be made righteous and would be purified. "My comrades," Booth wrote, "we must be ready for the New Heavens and the New Earth—new, indeed, to you and me because therein will dwell righteousness."[91] He envisioned that "the new earth will be for the special occupation and enjoyment of man. For, although he has cursed one world—oh, wonderful munificence!—God is to make him a present of another, for is it not to be a world wherein dwelleth righteousness—that is, righteous men and women?"[92]

As a result of personal righteousness "we shall have everywhere the good fruit of holy activities, and the example of a sweet and blessed life."[93] Booth referred to this righteousness alternately as inward purification, sanctification, or holiness, without which proper conduct was impossible, no matter how favorable people's physical surroundings were. Such righteousness was appropriate to the millennium. Booth wrote: "But in those days, by the power and operation of the Holy Spirit, the purpose of Christ, which is the destruction of the works of the devil, will be accomplished; men will be entirely sanctified, and the prophecy will be fulfilled which says 'Thy people shall all be righteous.'"[94]

However, in his later theology Booth thought of sanctification in corporate terms and categories, and not only personal ones. This was also true of sanctification in the millennium. He believed that the natural result of personal righteousness would be corporate righteousness—a righteous government administering just laws; a righteous business world conducting fair business practices; and a family reflecting wholesome relationships. The righteousness of the millennium would affect the relationships of people with people. There would be satisfactory institutional arrangements on the bases of mutual interest and mutual concern. This would be the case, for example, between employer and employee, or between capital and labor. "Goodness, and truth, and integrity will control every action of life."[95]

A third characteristic of the millennium was that love would prevail—people would love God, love their neighbors, and love themselves. Earth could be much like heaven, Booth believed, "by multiplying the number of loving hearts in it, whose chief care is not to protect their own rights and make others minister to their welfare, but who partake of the spirit of the Master, who came not to be ministered unto, but to minister, and left us the commandment that we should love one another even as He loved us. Verify it."[96] This is not love rooted in a general human understanding of love, which is not the love found in the Bible, but love rooted in the love of God and manifested in the incarnation. This love, like personal righteousness, would necessarily manifest itself in outward conduct. Booth understood this love to be a self-sacrificing love, similar in essence and in demonstration to the love shown by Booth's most important model, Jesus Christ. "And this same love flows through His broken heart, into the hearts of His fully surrendered people. Oh, blessed, patient, enduring, hoping, suffering love."[97]

Booth's imagery of battle and warfare was prevalent throughout his writings, and no less so when he was writing about love, for he envisioned love as, above all, victorious love. This love was such "that sees the misery-bleeding, God-dishonoring, and soul-destroying character of sin, and which, out of pity for its poor deluded victims, ever hates and opposes it."[98] In "A Passion For Souls" he wrote:

> Love must win. This is the mighty force of the future. This is the force that is going to drive sin and devils and misery out of the world, and own the Lord God Almighty as Sovereign in His own world. There are other forces. There is physical force, with its guns and bayonets, and dynamite, and the like. There is intellectual force, with its ideas and dreams, and books and orations, and I know not what; and there is the force of a burning affection which is greater than them all— the force of love—love that suffers, and sacrifices and dies—the force that has its origin in the heart of Jesus Christ, nay, a higher source than that—for this is the river that flows from the very heart of God Himself.[99]

The goal of this love was similar to the goal of personal righteousness—to seek the happiness of all people in the new kingdom. In *Religion For Every Day*, Booth wrote:

> What is the sum of celestial happiness, the happiness of God, the happiness of the Angels, the happiness of the Blood-washed spirits who are safely landed there? In what does this happiness chiefly consist?
>
> I reply, Not in the golden streets, the unfading flowers, the marvelous music, nor all the other wonders of the Celestial Land put together, but in Love. Love is the essence of the bliss of Heaven, for "Love is Heaven, and Heaven is Love." This happiness we can have below. It is not the love others bear to us that makes our felicity, but the love we bear to them; and, thank God, we can as truly love on earth as we can in Heaven .... Where this principle is carried into effect, every part of human conduct becomes religious—nay, a positive act of Divine worship, and an acceptable song of praise.[100]

This kind of love, Booth believed, would pragmatically influence relationships among people that would lead to mutual interest and concern. Characterizing this love as "in partnership with Divine love,"[101] he foresaw the actions of people living in the Kingdom of God in this way: "All loving and laboring for the happiness of each other, and that the more eagerly as any may be weak, or erring, or friendless. Thus will all be living, not in selfish competition as to who can most effectually advance his own personal interests even though it be to the damage of his neighbour, but seeking how most effectually to promote the interest of the whole."[102] Without this love any concept of the kingdom and the millennium was quite impossible for Booth. He asked:

> And again, when or where can you have any sort of a Millennium without love? What is wanted is that men should love one another, and that will end the poverty, and injustice, and cold-shouldering of misery, which is one of the worst forms that injustice assumes among men. Love is the mainspring, the only great moving force of all rightly constructed society.[103]

A fourth characteristic of the millennium was one that has been hinted at in the above characteristics—that of human happiness. This was important for Booth, who insisted that "the inhabitants of that New World will be Happy."[104] It was important in the later theology of William Booth to hold that the present miseries of people would be abolished during the millennium. His theology required a resolution of the problem of evil, but it required especially an end to human misery and suffering, caused by such forces as the wickedness of parents, crime, vices, evil passions, drunkenness, poverty, hunger, disease, and the inflictions caused by selfishness, greed, hatred, jealousies, envyings, and revenge. The millennium was, among other things, a time when "God shall rend the heavens and come down, and this mountain shall flow down at His presence, and the place whereon it stands shall know it no more, and instead of its misery there shall be happiness, instead of its groans and gnashing of teeth, there shall be songs of gladness."[105]

A fifth characteristic of the millennium was the literal, physical transformation of the present world. Booth understood the biblical nature of the Kingdom of God in these literalistic and physical terms, and was convinced that "we are going to have a NEW WORLD."[106] One of the first signs of the transformed millennial world would be an abundant supply of earthly needs in an atmosphere where people would live in harmony with God and in a spirit of goodwill with other people. This would be communal living in the truest sense. "He that hath more than he needs will, out of his abundance, gladly supply his brother's necessity; and he will do this, not only of his own free will, but in the acting out of his own loving nature."[107]

Another sign of that new world would be the encouragement of vocation. Booth insisted that work would be part of millennial living here on earth. His Victorian sense of vocation pervaded even his theology of the Kingdom of God, and work during the millennium would be done willingly and with a great deal of care and attention. He believed that work well done was honorable to God. He also believed that it was gratifying for an honest laborer to look upon his or her life's work from day to day, and he did not see this as in any way inconsistent with millennial living. In summarizing his position of the satisfaction of good work in the millennium in concert with the godly attitude that motivates a person to good work and good action, Booth stated:

> Now take all these things together, and a great many
> more which they suggest on the same lines, and tell
> me, dear reader, whether you do not think that when
> God really reigns on this earth, when every heart has
> been cleansed, and every life has been rectified, and
> every bosom flows with the loving spirit of Jesus Christ,
> we shall not have a very enjoyable world—an all but
> universal Paradise. Blotted and imperfect it may be,

with much infirmity still existing, yet very nearly akin
to heaven itself it must surely be. Though we may not
have circumstances and surroundings as favorable to
happiness as will be found in that blessed land, yet
surely we shall have that which has infinitely more to
do with happiness than circumstances and surroundings; we shall possess the character and the spirit of the
God of heaven, which must constitute its chiefest and
most rapturous joy."[108]

Another sign of this transformed world was in Booth's curi-
ously imaginative speculation that the center of the millennium
would be London and England. His eschatology reflected not only
institutional loyalties, but national loyalties as well. William Booth
was a loyal subject of the British empire of the nineteenth century,
and his nationalistic sympathies and allegiances can be seen running through his writings. And eventually officialdom responded
in kind to Booth's loyalty.[109]

This was no more in evidence than when, in an interview with
King Edward VII, the king said to Booth: "You are doing a great
work, General Booth, the success of which I regard as of great
importance to my Empire."[110] Booth tended to visualize his England
as a nation that had potential for evil or for good. Sometimes he
feared that England would go to hell "unless we can awaken it in
time."[111] He said the following in an article entitled "Rise and Fall"
for *The Christian Mission Magazine*: "Exalted to heaven with priv-
ileges, blessings, opportunities, and light, England will indeed go
down to hell, unless we can arouse and humble the people before
the King of all the Earth. Was there ever a nation more clearly
convicted of forgetting God than ours?"[112]

However, he was basically favorably disposed toward England,
and when he conceived of the millennium in terms of physical
transformation, he envisioned London as the model. Indeed,
London would become the New Jerusalem. In one article he articulated that "Oh London, that ought to be the New Jerusalem in this

lower world."[113] In another article he attempted to imagine what London would be like after the millennial transformation. In this visionary conception he said about London that:

> First, we should have Hyde Park roofed in, with towers climbing toward the stars, as THE WORLD'S GREAT GRAND CENTRAL TEMPLE. Only think what this would mean. And then, what demonstrations, what processions, what mighty assemblies, what grand reviews, what crowded streets, impassable with the joyful multitudes marching to and fro.
>
> The bells of Saint Paul's and Westminster Abbey and every other sanctuary, together with the trumpet calls from the roof of every Salvation Army barracks, would announce to the people the hours of prayer and praise. Methinks that at the summons for the 12:30 Daily Service the whole city would be prostrate, business and traffic, buying and selling, discussions and conversations, would all cease, and for a season the Five Million hearts, whether in home or factory, shop or exchange, warehouse or street, would turn to God with the voice of thanksgiving and with shouts of praise.[114]

This New Jerusalem would exist without jails, because there would be no more law-breakers; without courts, because there would be no more offenders; and without police, except those who would be needed to act "as officers of order to the multitudes who will come from every part of the globe to see the glory of God in His Great Temple."[115] There would be no cruelty to men, women, children, or animals; no poverty, because industry and economy would be practiced by everyone; no workhouses, no pauperism; and "slumdom with its wretched denizens will be no more."[116]

Nor would the transformed world need hospitals or lunatic asylums, because disease will have been eliminated "by moderation, frugality, and happiness."[117] Above all, in this New Jerusalem a spirit of love and sympathy would prevail among people. Booth envisioned that "In the houses, shops, factories, and exchanges; in the parks, fields, and streets; nay, everywhere men and women and little children will greet each other, help each other, bless each other, with hearts overflowing with this heavenly, Godlike spirit of love."[118]

The sixth characteristic of the millennium was that the final triumph of godliness over evil would be ushered in by the personal reign of Christ. "That will be a wonderful moment when He comes in the clouds of Heaven," Booth wrote in 1912, "and when, on the judgment seat, He summons the world before Him."[119] However, the establishment of the millennium would precede that final triumph and would be characterized spiritually "by further and mightier outpourings of the Holy Ghost than any yet known."[120] The millennium would be the time of working out a complete reconciliation of people with their world, of people with people, and of people with God. When that reconciliation was accomplished, Christ would come again and personally reign.

It needs to be reiterated in order to understand this aspect of the later theology of William Booth—Booth was increasingly convinced that The Salvation Army was the special agent of this Kingdom of God. He was sure that if people everywhere would follow the principles laid down by him and share his hope for the future, this would go "a long way towards bringing in the millennium."[121] His institutional loyalties were shared by many of those who were members of the hierarchy of The Salvation Army, and who envisioned the Kingdom of God and the millennium in the same ways, ways which in turn legitimated the work of the organization and its hierarchical structure. Booth's millennial dreams were shared dreams.[122]

Christian Ethics

Before leaving this second stage in the theology of William Booth, some word needs to be said about his Christian ethics. As in his first stage, his ethics were still very much personalized. Individual, private ethics were still important. However, Booth's theology was evolving in such a way that he drew institutional implications from his theology. During this stage in his theology, Booth entered somewhat into the arena of social ethics.

Both his movement and he were becoming increasingly aware both of social and institutional evils and of the need to respond to those evils in ways that transcended personal ethical concerns or private charitable actions. So, for example, the involvement of Catherine Booth, Bramwell Booth, and W. T. Stead in the alleviation of the white slave trade in England in the mid 1880s forced Booth and others to see the necessity of institutional responses to the prevailing evils of society.

Booth's social ethics would come into clearer focus once he had developed a theological system that embraced social redemption. That theology constituted a third stage in the theology of William Booth, and the next chapter of this analysis will deal with that third stage.

CHAPTER III

Stage Three: The Ministry and Theology of William Booth from 1889-1890

The most significant and dramatic change in the later theology of William Booth was an evolution that included an understanding of salvation as not only personal, but social as well. The interpretation of this process of change requires probing three interlocking areas: the ministry of William Booth, the expanding focus of his later theology of redemption, and the chronological context in which this change developed.

Booth's later theology of salvation was articulated after The Salvation Army had increased its activity to include the dual mission of personal salvation and social salvation. This grew out of social sensitivities that were evident in both Booth and The Christian Mission before the founding of The Salvation Army and led toward the second mission undertaken by The Salvation Army.

This will serve to explain Booth's later theology of salvation. It will also explain when that theology came to focus. It will be shown in this third section that Booth focused his theology of social salvation from 1889 to 1890. The first task of this chapter, however, is to explain the context of the change in the theology of William Booth, and this chapter now will move to that task.

The Ministry of William Booth

Historical Roots of Expanding Mission

It is clear, as expressed in Chapter I, that William Booth's major focus in his earlier theology reflected his revivalism. His theology evolved, however, to include a double mission. The theme of redemption had always been central to his theology and preaching, but eventually that theme incorporated social redemption as well as personal redemption. Likewise, the practice of Booth's Army evolved to embrace the mission of social redemption, having engaged in the work of personal redemption since Christian Mission days. By 1890, The Salvation Army and William Booth were well launched on a dual mission. The events leading up to that theological shift must be considered. These preliminary observations demonstrate that Booth's social sensitivities were evident in his life even since his time in Nottingham, and that The Christian Mission embraced a second form of activity for a short period of time, organized for all Christian Mission stations.

Booth was thoroughly exposed to and immersed in the life of industrial Nottingham. His father died when William was only thirteen, and as the only surviving son of the family William Booth had to make ends meet for his mother, sisters, and himself by an apprenticeship to a pawnbroker, a trade in which he witnessed the desperation of people to meet their daily needs. There is no indication from any of the biographers of Booth that this period in his life was marked by anything other than poverty, and the nineteenth year of his life was the lowest point of this time. He was out of work for a year.

He and his closest friend, one Will Sansom, showed a penchant for two activities on Sundays and in the evenings after work—they enjoyed conducting religious street meetings, and they assisted some of the less fortunate people whom they met on the streets of Nottingham. "Will Sansom and he rescued a tatterdemalion old woman from the extremity of poverty and put her in a cabin and provided for her.[1] The importance of noting such instances in Booth's life in Nottingham is not only the fact that he early on demonstrated some genuine sensitivity toward people less fortunate than his family. William Booth was somewhat of a preacher. He was also compassionate upon poor people, and that compassion would be one of his finest characteristics throughout his lifetime. It never diminished, but only increased with time and experience. Precisely how he channeled that compassion will be noted.

During the time of his relationship with New Connexion Methodism and of his independent ministry from 1861 to 1865, his attention was given to preaching to sinners and converting sinners. This was, as has been noted in Chapter I, his only emphasis. With the founding of what was to be known as The Christian Mission in 1865, that resolve initially remained unchanged.

However, a second form of activity entered into the programs of the preaching stations of The Christian Mission, and the first official Report of The Christian Mission, written in September of 1867, demonstrates that the Christian Missioners were conducting house to house visitation, running Sabbath and day schools, establishing maternal societies, and supplying clothes for the needy. The "Programme of the East London Christian Mission" was part of that report, and reveals that the weekly schedule included writing, reading, and arithmetic classes, a Drunkards' Rescue Society, and the opening of a savings bank.[2] Ministries were conducted by the local Christian Mission stations as there was need.

Perhaps the most popular expression of the desire to bless people in body as well as soul was the establishment of soup kitchens, and there were as many as five food shops operated by the Mission with "Food for the Million" as a slogan set up to feed the poor for a price in 1870. This was not gratuitous feeding for free, but was feeding designed to provide inexpensive and nourishing meals for the poor. This was the one social ministry that was organized for all the stations. These feeding stations were placed under the control of Bramwell Booth, who was ably assisted by one James

Flawn, a Christian Mission convert and one who had been in the food service business before joining the Mission. However, eventually these soup kitchens had to be closed for lack of funds, the last feeding station being closed in 1874. In fact, the general relief work of the Mission could no longer be undertaken by the Mission by 1877. "General relief work seems later to have been abandoned by The Christian Mission, for writing to the Rev. Arthur Wedgwood (hon. secretary of the Whitechapel Union Division of the Charity Organization Society) in June 1877 William Booth stated that the Mission had ceased almost entirely to administer relief to strangers, but instead referred them to the Charity Organization Society."[3]

The first and primary involvement of The Christian Mission continued to be the preaching of the Gospel to sinners, and Booth's writings at this time reflect that priority. Booth's theology was still being developed, and there was no sign yet of Booth's application of theological terms such as salvation or redemption to the physical realities around him. Salvation was still primarily salvation of the soul, and not yet social salvation, as would be envisioned and articulated in Booth's later theology.

The Second Mission of The Salvation Army

Adherence to a single mission would remain true for Booth up to the change of the name of The Christian Mission to The Salvation Army in 1878 and well into the time of the development of The Salvation Army. In explaining the name change from The Christian Mission to The Salvation Army, Booth affirmed this single mission. "We are a Salvation people—this is our specialty—getting saved and keeping saved, and then getting somebody else saved, and then getting saved ourselves more and more, until full salvation on earth makes the heaven within, which is finally perfected by the full salvation without, on the other side of the river .... My brethren, my comrades, soul saving is our avocation, the great purpose and business of our lives. Let us seek first the kingdom of God, let us be SALVATIONISTS indeed."[4]

78

In presenting the work of The Salvation Army to the Wesleyan Conference in August of 1880, Booth stated that "We go on the three broad lines of Repentance, Faith, and Holiness of Heart."[5] One would search in vain in this entire address in which he set forth the principles of The Salvation Army, and many similar addresses at this stage in Booth's theology, to find any reference to soup kitchens or lodging houses, let alone any theological justification for the extended ministry of social salvation. William Booth and his Salvation Army were still involved in the single ministry of converting sinners. That, it was thought, was the highest service that could be rendered to the poor.

However, others in the movement began to recognize the complexity of their ministry, and there dawned an awareness in some of Booth's officers and soldiers that it was not enough to preach the Gospel to the poor, but that preaching had to be complemented by taking care of the physical needs of the poor to whom they preached. And so it is a fact of history that the organized social work of The Salvation Army did not begin at the initiation of William Booth in East London, but with Salvationists in Melbourne, Australia in 1883 with the establishment of a half-way home for released prisoners. The center was opened on December 8, 1883. Previous to this, in May of that year, a rescue home for women was opened in Glasgow, Scotland, but that home was evidently closed by March of 1884. Therefore, it is Australia that holds the distinction of beginning the sustained organized social work of The Salvation Army.

It was not until May 1884 that social work began in an organized fashion in Booth's back yard, as it were. A rescue home for prostitutes was opened at Hanbury Street, Whitechapel, at the instigation of a soldier of The Salvation Army, one Mrs. Cottrill. From evidence gleaned from the operation of this home, and with the encouragement and support of the journalist W. T. Stead, the Booths and the Army became involved in 1884-1885 with the issue of the white slave trade and prostitution in England, and were influential in raising the age of consent for girls from thirteen to sixteen.

In the meantime, various officers and soldiers continued to involve themselves in diverse aspects of social work. In Toronto, Ontario, Canada in 1886, the Army opened the first institution to give special attention to alcoholic women, and in 1887 there was the opening of a day care center in one of the "slum posts" of London (Borough) so that working mothers could have provision for their children during hours of employment. The crippling London dock strike of 1888 "tested the faith of settlers and Salvationists who responded with sympathy, enthusiasm, and practical aid."[6] A food and shelter center for the homeless was established on the West India Dock Road. In 1889 a women's shelter was opened on Hanbury Street, and on June 29, 1890 The Salvation Army opened the first "Elevator", a "sheltered workshop"[7] for men.

However, until 1889 Booth was still making no public pronouncements about these social operations. He was not condemning these operations, and was apparently pleased with the initiative that his people were showing. But his theology still reflected only a single purpose for his Army—that of winning souls. A typical article of Booth's is found in *The War Cry* in January 1887 which he wrote after a thirteen-week journey of 16,000 miles. In that article he wrote:

> I have come back with the impression that the need of the world was bigger than ever I thought it was, and I have also come back with the impression that The Salvation Army is equal to it, if The Salvation Army will only do its duty.[8]

In the entire article, Booth made no reference to a second mission, to social salvation, to social work. His references were only to the soul-saving mission of The Salvation Army and to spiritual redemption.

The magnitude of the social problems that The Salvation Army was addressing came to sharp focus during the middle 1880s in England, and it was during this time that Booth's sensitivity to the poor to whom he had been preaching for many years was heightened through the experiences of his Army. By the middle eighties a severe economic depression had taken its toll on England, and the affects of that depression manifested themselves in the places where Booth's Army was at work, "1873 being the date normally given for the beginning of the 'great depression' and 1874 as the beginning of the nineteenth century disaster to British agriculture."[9]

A serious analysis of poverty, homelessness, unemployment, and religion in the East End of London entitled *Life and Labour in the East of London* was written by Charles Booth in 1883, and was eventually expanded into the seventeen-volume work entitled *Life and Labour of the People of London,* of which Volume One was published before William Booth published his *In Darkest England and the Way Out.* William Booth made use of Charles Booth's work, and was impressed with the sad plight of the people with whom the Army and he had been working and to whom the Gospel had been preached.

Finally, it was decided that an office be created to deal with the social reform operations of The Salvation Army. Therefore, by 1890 these thus far tentative efforts of The Salvation Army at social reform were placed under the office of what became known as the Social Reform Wing of The Salvation Army, commanded by Commissioner Frank Smith.

With the establishment of the Social Reform Wing, The Salvation Army entered into a new stage in its ministry. It finally recognized institutionally the importance of the second mission that had gradually gained acceptance. Between 1889 and 1890 the commitment to social salvation became fixed. This time was significant in the history of The Salvation Army. Hitherto its chief concern had been for personal salvation from sin, and social concerns were secondary, but increasing in importance. Now, however, the movement was engaged in two works—personal salvation and social salvation. It now had, as has been mentioned, a dual mission. It now was engaged in war on two fronts.

The surest expression of this mission came from Booth himself. In October 1890 Booth published *In Darkest England and the Way Out* in which he gave theological expression to the necessity of social salvation in which The Salvation Army had already been engaged. A description of that work as well as its significance will be treated later in this chapter.

Some Reasons for Entering into a Second Mission

The question needs to be asked: why did the transition take place, and why was Booth ready to focus his enlarged vision of salvation and of a double mission? Indeed, W. T. Stead himself, who assisted Booth in the writing of *In Darkest England and the Way Out*, stated in *The Star* on January 2, 1891: "Everyone knows perfectly well that two years ago, nay, even one year ago, General Booth did not see his way to the utilization of The Salvation Army as an instrument of social reform."[10]

There are many possible answers to this question, and many factors, both personal and institutional, coalesced at this time and gave rise to an expanded ministry. The first has already been noted many times, but bears repeating. Booth always demonstrated social sensitivities, especially toward the poor and needy, which were evident in Nottingham, in Whitechapel Road, and in the ministry of The Salvation Army. However, at one time these social interests were fleeting compared with his concern for the personal conversion of men and women. Experience, both personal and institutional, had heightened his sensitivities about people's physical plights. He personally wanted to do well by people.

This heightened sensitivity was shared with many who had joined Booth's Salvation Army, and culminated in the 1880s with Booth's and The Salvation Army's continual exposure to the stark realities of depressed urban life both in London and in other parts of the world. The experiences gained by Booth and the Social Reform Wing, especially in the context of a great depression in England in the 1880s, caused them to come to grips with the fact that people were not interested in an escapist gospel, but welcomed a gospel that sustained them physically as well as spiritually. W. T. Stead himself noted that the experience gained by the increasing social wing of The Salvation Army "encouraged the General to take a decided step in advance."[11]

Added to this, William Booth certainly recognized that virtually hundreds of other people and organizations were engaged in social work.[12] Much of the work of England was under the auspices of an agency known as the Charity Organization Society, a group that consequently saw no need for the Army's social work, and often opposed such work. The work, so claimed the Charity Organization Society, was already being done. However, if the reports of Charles Booth were correct, the work was inadequate and certainly was not having any lasting results, especially in the arena of the serious problem of unemployment and other attendant problems. Booth, believing that he was now ready to improve on the work being done, offered the following criticism:

> And yet all the way through my career I have keenly felt the remedial measures usually enunciated in Christian programmes and ordinarily employed by Christian philanthropy to be lamentably inadequate for any effectual dealing with the despairing miseries of these outcast classes. The rescued are appallingly few—a ghastly minority compared with the multitudes who struggle and sink in the open-mouthed abyss. Alike, therefore, my humanity and my Christianity, if I may speak of them in any way as separate one from the other, have cried out for some more comprehensive method of reaching and saving the perishing crowds.[13]

Third, much of the Church demonstrated an unwillingness to enter into a second mission, and by 1890 Booth, convinced that it was theologically correct to address the issue of social redemption systematically, was willing to commit himself in a way which he wished for the Church. He was at times critical of the Church for not understanding the necessity of or the nature of social redemption. "Why all this apparatus of temples and meetinghouses to save men from perdition in a world which is to come, while never a helping hand is stretched out to save them from the inferno of their present life?[14]

Also important to Booth was the authoritarian structure of the Army, which was well in place and functioning by 1889. Booth related that structure to his second mission—he believed that his organization was best suited for redemption in two worlds because of its authoritarian structure. The dual redemptive mission of The Salvation Army would succeed through proper management where other less authoritarian or individualistic enterprises had failed. He wrote that "so far from resenting the exercise of authority, The Salvation Army rejoices to recognize it as one great secret of its success, a pillar of strength upon which all its soldiers can rely, a principle which stamps it as being different from all other religious organizations founded in our day."[15]

Another possible reason why Booth was now ready to enter into this second mission revolved around the changing influential persons in his life and ministry. As has been noted, two significant persons in Booth's life were Catherine Booth and George Scott Railton. Both were adamant that the primary work of the ministry—the chief work of The Christian Mission and The Salvation Army—was the conversion of sinners and the raising up of saints. However, there was a diminishing influence of these people upon Booth with Catherine Booth's death in 1890 and with Railton's continuing lack of sympathy with the growing social emphasis of The Salvation Army, climaxing with his protestations in 1894 of the launching of The Salvation Army Assurance Society.[16]

Catherine Booth had been ill for quite some time previous to 1890, and her influence in the Army was chiefly in the realm of encouraging the officers and soldiers, and preaching and teaching such doctrines as holiness and the role of women in ministry.

This is not to say that she did not have sympathy with this second mission. She was a chief player in the Purity Crusade of 1885. And William Booth consulted her on the writing of *In Darkest England* and dedicated the book to her. However, it remains a moot question of precisely how critical Catherine Booth would have been of the new direction of redemption once she saw it fully inaugurated.

On the other hand, Railton at this same period of time was a tireless itinerant evangelist, opening up the work of The Salvation Army in many parts of the world and guiding such work, and was therefore far removed from Booth and the organizational and administrative development of The Salvation Army in London. Those closest to Booth in the development of the Darkest England Scheme were Bramwell Booth, W. T. Stead, and Frank Smith. Bramwell Booth, the eldest son and Chief of the Staff, had long been convinced of the necessity of social ministries. W. T. Stead was a journalist whose personal sympathies were for the betterment of society by many possible means, not the least of which was the work of The Salvation Army. He helped Booth with the writing of *In Darkest England and the Way Out*. Frank Smith, ever advancing the social programs of the Army, was the commissioner in charge of the Social Reform Wing of The Salvation Army before the Darkest England Scheme was proposed to the public.

Thus, by late 1890 The Salvation Army was well launched on a second mission. It was now a movement that was committed to both spiritual redemption and social redemption. Likewise, by late 1890 William Booth had developed a doctrine of redemption that embraced both spiritual and social redemption.

William Booth's Later Theology of Redemption
Personal Salvation from Sin

Corresponding to this watershed in activity one finds a shift in the theology of William Booth. This section of the chapter will probe his later theology of redemption, and the next section of the chapter will examine precisely when Booth formulated this later theology of redemption.

This is vitally important when examining Booth's later theology of redemption: it is incorrect to say that the social concerns of Booth in his later life diminished his doctrine of justification by faith for the individual. This was still a theme with Booth in his later years. His later theology of redemption still embraced his belief that Jesus Christ came into the world for the basic work of redemption and atonement. Even in his later theology he did not develop an elaborate theology of justification by faith or atonement, nor did he deal with the many nuances of these doctrines. He was, however, still sure of this: since the fall people needed to be at one again with God, and people could not accomplish this themselves because of their rebellion against God. Therefore, God came to earth in the person of Jesus Christ, and by dying on the cross in the place of all sinners, Jesus Christ both satisfied God's demand for justice, and showed forth God's love for humanity.

The necessity laid upon each individual was personal repentance of sins and personal faith in Jesus Christ. This emphasis upon faith, upon the will of people lost at the fall but restored by God's prevenient grace, upon people's consent toward their own salvation, was constant throughout Booth's theology, and it was present still in his later theology of redemption. As late as May 18, 1912 he wrote an article entitled "Will You Let Me In?" in which he stated:

> He wants to come to bless you. But He cannot come in without your consent. There is the condition. He has made you a free agent. You have the power to keep Him out. That is almost as wonderful as He wanting to come in. He cannot come in if there remain lusts, devils, filthy passions in your soul. What can I do with them? Open the door and let Him in and He will soon sweep them out; they will fly at His presence.[17]

Social Salvation from Evil

The critical change in the theology of William Booth came when his doctrine of salvation took on social dimensions. In his later theology of redemption, salvation was not only individual, personal, and spiritual. Salvation was also social and physical. Accentuating the imagery of Christ as the model soldier, Booth insisted that Christ came to earth not only to die on the cross, but to be raised from the dead. And in his resurrection he conquered such unholy alliances as evil and death and initiated the redemption of the whole world—spiritual and physical.

This being the case, it was necessary for believers to follow their model, and to take the side of the conquering Christ in the work of redemption of the world. The dimensions and dynamics of salvation were both personal and social. Christ, therefore, was "the Deliverer,"[18] and the will of God and of Christ was not only that personal sin be destroyed, but "that devils should be sent back to hell."[19]

He applied the language of salvation to social redemption. He held that people could enjoy spiritual salvation by faith, and he likewise believed that people could enjoy physical salvation from the evils that beset them in this earthly life. "As Christ came to call not saints but sinners to repentance, so the New Message of Temporal Salvation, of salvation from pinching poverty, from rags and misery, must be offered to all."[20]

The Possibility of Universal Social Redemption

Upon one point Booth became absolutely insistent—there was the possibility of personal and social salvation for every person, and therefore there was the possibility of complete spiritual and social redemption. Because he believed in the possibility of universal redemption, he found himself opposed to any doctrine that taught that salvation was limited to the elect of God. Catherine Booth once wrote that "he believed that there had been an ATONEMENT made, sufficient for every sinner, and that by true repentance and faith in the Lord Jesus Christ, the very worst might enter upon a new life."[21] Booth wrote of himself that he was "thrown, almost at the onset of my religious career, over head and ears as it were, into the Calvinistic Controversy; but I was strengthened, perhaps, in my views of Human Responsibility as to the outcome."[22]

To reiterate—nowhere was the theme of the universality of salvation more important to the later theology of Booth than in his understanding that salvation included social, as well as personal, reclamation. If spiritual salvation was limited, it followed naturally that social salvation was also limited, and that the mission of the Church in social salvation was seriously hindered. He wrote:

> No one will ever make a visible dint on the Mass of Squalor who does not deal with the improvident, the lazy, the vicious, and the criminal. The Scheme of Social Salvation is not worth discussion which is not as wide as the Scheme of Eternal Salvation set forth in the Gospel. The Glad Tidings must be to every creature, not merely to an elect few who are to be saved while the mass of their fellows are predestined to a temporal damnation. We have had this doctrine of an inhuman cast-iron pseudo-political economy too long enthroned amongst us. It is now time to fling down the false idol, and proclaim a Temporal Salvation as full, free, and universal, and with no other limitations than the "Whosoever will" of the Gospel.[23]

However, Booth maintained a consistency theologically in his view of the universality of the gospel. He held that just as people could by willful consent reject personal salvation from sin, so people could by willful consent reject social salvation. The responsibility rested with those to whom either gospel had been preached. "But we who call ourselves by the name of Christ are not worthy to profess to be His disciples until we have set an open door before the least and worst of these who are now apparently imprisoned for life in a horrible dungeon of misery and despair. The responsibility for its rejection must be theirs, not ours."[24]

These, then, were the primary characteristics of Booth's later doctrine of redemption: his later theology of redemption still included personal salvation from sin for the individual who believes; his later theology of redemption developed in such a way that it included social salvation from the evils that beset people in this world; and just as there was the possibility of universal spiritual redemption (i.e., salvation was not limited to the elect), so there was the possibility of universal social redemption. People were, however, responsible for either accepting or rejecting the offer of salvation.

The Timing of William Booth's Later Theology of Redemption
"Salvation for Both Worlds"

William Booth's theology of salvation underwent a dramatic transition from 1889 to 1890. That theology was expressed first in one of his most important articles, and then in one of the most important books that he wrote. The first instance of his changed theology of salvation is found in an article appropriately entitled "Salvation for Both Worlds," published in *All The World* in January 1889. That article is illuminating for four reasons.

First, this article is subtitled "A Retrospect," and in it Booth looks back to his forty-four years of serving God. He speaks of his growing awareness of the miseries of people to whom he was preaching—those who were hungry, drunk, absorbed in all kinds of vices and abominations. "I saw poor women and children compelled to live in hovels of the most wretched squalor and filth, from which light and air were all but excluded. I saw the people dying prematurely of disease from the want of food and attention. I knew that thousands of young women were being sacrificed to the gratification of the lusts of men who bought and sold them, body and soul, for the most paltry prices."[25] Booth was likewise stricken by the fact that those who had the means to help the poor were indifferent to their needs, and he loathed the unjust laws "that seemed to favor the perpetuation of the calamitous circumstances that pressed so heavily on the wretched multitudes."[26]

However, the experience of the ministry of the past forty-four years among the poor caused Booth eventually to comprehend a gospel that included salvation for both worlds. Frederick Coutts' observation of the initiation of social ministry in a full scale could be said of William Booth as well of the Salvationists of that time: "The Army's social services were not born out of any doctrinaire theory but out of the involvement of the Salvationist himself in situations of human need."[27] William Booth expressed in this article the culmination of his thinking to this point, the full illumination, as it were, of his understanding of the many dimensions of the gospel. He expressed himself with this language:

> Now I shouted, "I have found the remedy indeed!" Now I saw that this was the work that Jesus Christ came to accomplish—that he was manifested to dispossess all these fiends of evil from the souls of men, to destroy the work of the devil in the present time, and to set up in the soul the kingdom of heaven instead.
>
> And I said to myself, and I have been saying to others ever since, "Christ is the deliverer for time as truly as for eternity. He is the Joshua who leads men in our own day out of the wilderness into the promised land, as His forerunner did the children of Israel thousands of years ago. He is the Messiah who brings glad tidings! He is come to open the prison doors. He is come to set men free from their bonds. He is indeed the Saviour of the world! Men can have liberty, gladness here and now through Him, and I will consecrate my life to persuade them to apply to him for the deliverance that He came to bring.[28]

Second, Booth admitted that, although he had always been aware of the physical impoverishment of the people to whom he had preached, having experienced poverty himself, he nevertheless initially, at the outset of his ministry, saw no remedy for that, "and I said to myself, 'If we cannot save them for time, we will save them for eternity!' The very thought that there was no lightening of their lot in time, quickened and stimulated me in seeking to brighten their condition in eternity."[29] He would, by his own admission, learn otherwise as time went on.

Third, his experiences with the poor had provided him with an education. He became aware of the physical and institutional dimensions of evil. He gradually learned from experience "that the miseries from which I sought to save man in the next world were substantially the same as those from which I everywhere found him suffering in this."[30] He broadened his doctrinal understanding and his theological language to take into account his own changed theology. Experience had shaped his theology in such a way that he now conceived of hell not only as a place of endless punishment for the wicked, of which alienation from God in this life was a sign, but he now wrote of the outward hell of "poverty, drunkenness, debauchery, crime, slavery, war, and every other form of outward misery."[31]

Lastly, concomitant with his heightened awareness of evil, was a belief that he now had two gospels to preach—a gospel of redemption from personal sin and a gospel of redemption from social evil. Again, he broadened his theological language to take into account his changed theology. He added new dimension and new meaning to the theological language that he had been expressing for years. Salvation was now social as well as personal. Booth wrote:

> But with this discovery, there also came another, which has been growing and growing in clearness and intensity from that hour to this; which was that I had two gospels of deliverance to preach—one for each world, or rather, one gospel which applied alike to both. I saw that when the Bible said, "He that believeth shall

be saved," it meant not only saved from the miseries
of the future world, but from the miseries of this also.
That it came with the promise of salvation here and
now; from hell and sin and vice and crime and idleness
and extravagance, and consequently very largely from
poverty and disease, and the majority of kindred foes.[32]

In Darkest England and the Way Out

Ten months after the writing of "Salvation for Both Worlds,"
designed obviously to prepare his own people for a personal and
institutional allegiance to and commitment to a double mission,
Booth began writing *In Darkest England and the Way Out*. The
Salvation Army had already demonstrated both a willingness and
a capability to enter into social ministries. William Booth was
convinced of the theological justification of both social salvation
and personal salvation, and with the writing of this book he was
now ready to commit his Salvation Army to war on two fronts.
He wrote *In Darkest England* to explain his developed theology
to the public, and thereby explain the evolution which had taken
place in his own thinking and in the mission of the Army that was
increasingly placing itself before the public eye. And the date of
the publication of *In Darkest England*, October 1890, was a critical date in the theology of William Booth because it most clearly
illustrates not only his broadened theological vision of redemption
to include social as well as personal categories, but it represents
his desire and his willingness to act in a way that was consistent
with his own theology.

In Darkest England was Booth's most extensive work and
proved to be his most widely read book, read not only by Salvationists but also by the general public for whom it was intended.
Once the book was published it did not escape notice. Neither
did it escape criticism. Booth had his critics, many of them caus-
tic, and some vitriolic. He also had his share of defenders. "As

Canon Dwyer pointed out, all of England became divided into Boothites and Anti-Boothites. Among Booth's sympathizers were Cardinal Manning, Archdeacon Farrer, Sir E. Clark (the Solicitor-General), and the Marquis of Queensberry; among his critics, Thomas Huxley, C. S. Loch (Secretary of the Charity Organization Society), Bernard Bosanquet, and Canon Dwyer. But even a critic like Dwyer had to admit that Booth had the right objectives in mind, although he was going about the matter quite wrongly.[33]

The book is basically Booth's description of his Darkest England Scheme, which was a crusade to assist the "submerged tenth"[34] of England's population, those whose lives were marked by poverty, homelessness, drunkenness, vice, prostitution, and any number of circumstances that kept these people from the security of work, income, home, family, or safety. Booth expected this scheme to help not only England but the world by providing a model of social salvation. Therefore, it was also necessary for Booth to articulate in the book his broadened view of redemption which now included social redemption. The redemptive theology that he had formulated provided the basis for the work that he outlined in the book.

Briefly, Booth built his Darkest England Scheme around what he called his Cab-Horse Charter, finding it a stigma and an enigma in nineteenth-century civilized society "that our horses are better treated than our labourers."[35] At the beginning of the book, he explained the charter in the following way:

> There are two points in the Cab Horse's Charter. When he is down he is helped up, and while he lives he has food, shelter, and work. That, although a humble standard, is at present unattainable by millions—literally by millions—of our fellow-men and women in this country. Can the Cab Horse Charter be gained for human beings? I answer, yes. The Cab Horse standard can be attained on the Cab Horse terms. If you get your fallen fellow on his feet again, Docility and Discipline will

enable you to reach the Cab Horse ideal, otherwise
it will remain unattainable. But Docility seldom fails
where Discipline is intelligently maintained.[36]

The first part of the book dealt with an analysis of the problems,
and this part he called "The Darkness." The second part of the book,
labeled "Deliverance," proposed solutions to the problems. These
solutions were divided among the city colony, the farm colony, and
the colony overseas, each colony designed to bring light to specific
aspects of England's darkness. Recognizing that other people and
other groups were proposing various plans to deal with the social
maladies of nineteenth-century England, Booth admitted that "All
that I want is to have the work done."[37] He wrote: "If you have any
better plan than mine for effecting this purpose, in God's name
bring it to the light and get it carried out quickly. If you have not,
then lend me a hand with mine, as I would be only too glad to lend
you a hand with yours if it had in it greater promise of successful
action than mine."[38]

It is important to note that Booth believed that his expanded
understanding of redemption was divinely blessed, as well as was
his plan to work in a way consistent with that understanding. He
held that this aspect of this theology, like all others, had roots "in
the very heart of God Himself."[39] It was necessary for him to hold
this. It was that conceptualization that provided ultimate theological legitimacy for the expanded and organized social work of The
Salvation Army after 1890. "I want it to be clearly understood,"
Booth wrote, "that it is not in my own strength, nor at my own
charge, that I purpose to embark upon this great undertaking.
Unless God wills that I should work out the idea of which I believe
He has given me the conception, nothing can come of any attempt
at its execution but confusion, disaster, and disappointment."[40]

This theme of divine blessing ran consistently throughout
the book, and was expressed in many ways. Restating this theme,
Booth wrote:

> But seeing that neither Governments, nor Society, nor
> individuals have stood forward to undertake what God
> has made appear to us to be so vitally important a work,
> and as He has given us the willingness, and in many
> important senses the ability, we are prepared . . . to
> make a determined effort, not only to undertake but
> to carry it forward to a triumphant success.[41]

The importance of *In Darkest England* to this study, however,
is to understand the book as it relates specifically to the change
in Booth's theology of redemption. In that light it is necessary to
point out that throughout the book, Booth struggled to explain the
relationship between personal and social salvation. It is true that
In Darkest England provided statistical data and institutional goals
that would help to alleviate the miseries of people. However, those
who read and interpret the book only in that light will seriously
miss an important intention of the book, and in doing so will mis-
interpret William Booth. The book is also, and at times primarily,
an expression of Booth's expanded conception of redemption.

Booth's theological intentions in the book were clear—he did
want to maintain the delicate balance between personal and social
salvation. Striking the balance became an important theme for
Booth in defending his conception of the place of social salvation
in the scheme of things, and in defending his expanded vision of
the participation of his Army in social redemption. The nature of
such a balance was important to Booth for at least two reasons.
First, he feared that social salvation would break loose from its ties
to spiritual salvation, thus rendering The Salvation Army merely
an ineffectual social agency. Second, he wanted to respond to his
critics on the one hand who denied the validity of his social work,
and his critics on the other hand who denied the validity of his
religious work. Booth was not equally clear, however, in spelling
out those intentions. There were times when his whole redemptive
picture included social redemption and personal redemption side
by side. Social and personal redemption were two sides of the same

coin. Social redemption was an equal and natural part of the whole redemptive picture, and it would ultimately help God redeem this world and establish a physical kingdom of God on earth.[42]

At other times, the imagery of redemption is different, and Booth goes to great lengths to explain that social salvation is not an end in itself, and that the work of The Salvation Army in the social realm was not an end in itself. Here Booth attempted to explain a natural order of redemption as he believed God had ordained it and as he understood it. The work of physical or social redemption was preparatory, necessarily, to the work of spiritual or personal redemption. Experience had taught him that people were so disastrously oppressed by their present physical circumstances that "these multitudes will not be saved in their present circumstances."[43]

Using the natural order of redemption as his imagery, Booth was convinced that "if these people are to believe in Jesus Christ, become the servants of God, and escape the miseries of the wrath to come, they must be helped out of their present social miseries."[44] He wrote:

> To change the nature of the individual, to get at the heart, to save his soul is the only real, lasting method of doing him any good. In many modern schemes of social regeneration it is forgotten that "it takes a soul to move a body, e'en to a cleaner sty," and at the risk of being misunderstood and misrepresented, I must assert in the most unqualified way that it is primarily and mainly for the sake of saving the soul that I seek the salvation of the body.[45]

This understanding of the natural order of redemption is evident in Booth's writings even outside of his *In Darkest England*.

In a letter to his officers years after the publication of *In Darkest England* he wrote:

But while you strive to deliver them from their temporal distresses, and endeavour to rescue them from
the causes that have led to their unfortunate condition,
you must seek, above all, to turn their miseries to good
account by making them help the salvation of their
souls and their deliverance from the wrath to come.
It will be a very small reward for all your toils if, after
bringing them into condition of well-being here, they
perish hereafter.[46]

In any case, there was a dramatic shift in the theology of
William Booth. Due to many forces, but primarily to his own
experience, the many experiences of Salvationists, and his own
developed theology, Booth's vision of redemption evolved from
solely personal and spiritual salvation to include also social and
physical redemption. Booth's theology of redemption was much
more inclusive in his later theology after 1889 than it had been
earlier, and, for better or for worse, Booth and his Army would
be perceived from that time onward as a man and a movement
engaged in social redemption on a much larger scale and with a
fuller vision of such redemption than had been present thus far in
either The Christian Mission or The Salvation Army.

An Invitation to Greater Understanding

A Call for a More Adequate Theological Awareness

It is hoped that this study has shed light on the theology of William Booth, on significant changes in that theology, and on the ministry of Booth as the primary context for the various stages in his theology. In the past, research that has been done on Booth has concentrated almost solely on the areas of history and biography, and has failed to take his theology into account.

This is beginning to change, and especially so during the past twenty years. For example, in the finest historical account to date of the work of The Salvation Army in America, *Marching to Glory* by Dr. Edward H. McKinley, the "militant redemptive theology"[1] of William Booth is acknowledged.

Theology was important to Booth, and it is hoped that this work will increase awareness of that fact. While William Booth was not a technically trained theologian, he nevertheless was guided by theological loyalties that were critical to him. A failure to understand that often leads to a serious misunderstanding of Booth and the movements which he and Catherine Booth founded. This often results in a misunderstanding of the impact which Booth and his Christian Mission and Salvation Army had upon the nineteenth century and the beginning of the twentieth century.

It has been argued throughout this study that the theology of William Booth changed, developed, and matured. Both the context of his theological formulations and his evolved theology are important in considering Booth's theology.

William Booth was first a nineteenth-century British revivalist, and his early theology reflected the context of his early ministry. He enjoyed a period of independent, revival ministry first with New Connexion Methodism and, after 1861, apart from New Connexion Methodism. His early theology demonstrated little change through his founding in 1865, along with Catherine Booth, of what became known as The Christian Mission. This would remain true up to 1878 with the evolution of The Christian Mission into The Salvation Army.

His emphasis upon personal theological categories was evident and clear in his preaching and his writing during this stage in his life. He was an Evangelical revival preacher, and along with the Evangelical community of nineteenth-century England, he stressed personal conversion from sin. However, he was not only an Evangelical, he was also Wesleyan. His theology included the Wesleyan doctrine of sanctification or perfect love. Booth applied the doctrines of salvation and sanctification to the individual, and he would continue to do so for the rest of his ministry. Although his theology evolved, it would still embrace such individual categories as personal redemption and personal sanctification.

There are nuanced changes in Booth's theology after the birth of The Salvation Army in 1878. Within that context, Booth added institutional categories and images to express his theology in order to include and incorporate the doctrinal changes that were taking place. Such extended theological language which accommodated his broadened theological views was common in much of Booth's theology after 1878, and this would continue to be true for the rest of his life. This fact is clearest as Booth's theology reflected his loyalty to a growing institution. After 1878, he understood the doctrine of sanctification in a broader way to include institutional sanctification. Not only were individuals made holy by God, but groups were also sanctified by God, and so he believed that his Salvation Army was especially blessed by the Holy Spirit.

For Booth, The Salvation Army became an Army sanctified by God and divinely ordained for the work of ultimate redemption. Military language increasingly served as a vehicle of expression for his theology, and Christ became the model salvation soldier, the model redeemer, in the war against evil. Booth's final eschatological vision—providing hope, direction, and legitimacy for his Army—was a fully redemptive vision in which sin and evil would ultimately be overcome. His eschatological goal embraced both spiritual and social redemption.

Many aspects of Booth's later redemptive theology provided a theological place of refuge for Booth and his followers, and the additions to his theology that he found so comforting and helpful continued to be pressed home the rest of his life. In fact, these changes would lend support to and complement Booth's most critical evolution in his theology, a change which allowed him to see redemption in social as well as personal dimensions.

It is beyond doubt that his developed redemptive theology, which was evident after 1889, constituted the most dramatic change in the theology of William Booth. This transformation was articulated after The Salvation Army had increased its activity to reflect a dual mission that included social redemption. This climaxed between 1889 and 1890 with the establishment of the Social Reform Wing of The Salvation Army.

Characteristic of this more nuanced theology, the very meaning of the word salvation evolved in Booth's thinking to include social salvation as well as personal salvation. Those who have written about Booth in the past have often been seriously mistaken both theologically and historically in holding that what moved William Booth principally when he saw the plight of Londoners living in East London in 1865 was their physical condition. What moved him was their spiritual condition—he saw them as sinners in rebellion against God. They affected his spiritual sensitivities, and he began his ministry among them as a revivalist and solely as a revivalist. At that time, salvation was personal and spiritual, and, convinced that people were sinners who needed such salvation, he called people to repentance, faith, and conversion.

However, as a result of his long ministry among the poor and the destitute, and after many years of personal experience within the context of The Christian Mission and The Salvation Army's social involvement, Booth would come to realize that salvation had social dimensions as well, and in 1889 he proposed a view of salvation that was sufficient to include both personal and spiritual dimensions. By 1889, the Army had already entered in many places upon a dual mission of saving sinners from their sin and redeeming the world from the evils that so beset it. After 1889, the Army engaged in its dual mission on a much larger scale and in the context of an organization for that dual mission that it had not previously established. Beyond that, William Booth provided theological legitimacy for such a dual mission, while at the same time he continually attempted to strike a proper balance between the salvation of the soul and the salvation of the body. However, after 1889 the Army was encouraged to see itself as engaged in a war on two fronts—the war for souls, and the war for a rightly ordered society.

As was mentioned in the Introduction, there were two problems that constantly surfaced when trying to define the theology of Booth and when attempting to discern the maturing of that theology. First, there was often a lack of theological precision in his writings and his speaking. This lack of precision may cause some confusion about the exact intentions or directions of his theology. Booth was not always critically aware of how theology is formulated or of how or why theology changes. Also, his writing and preaching was done primarily for the faithful Christian Missioners and Salvationists and not for the wider scholarly world. It is especially important that the contexts of his statements be taken into account. Likewise, it has sometimes been necessary to impose an order on Booth's theology in order to deal systematically and critically with his theology and with the changes which ensued in its evolution.

The second problem is connected with the first, to which allusion has already been made. Booth was not always aware of how theology is formulated. He was not always clear about the sources which he was using for his doctrinal statements. He likewise was not always cognizant of subtle changes which were taking place in his own thinking. In brief, he was not trained to take a critical and objective look at his own shaping of theology.

A Call for a More Accurate Interpretive Perspective

In the past, there have been three distinct failures in attempting to understand William Booth and thereby place him in proper perspective.

First, many scholars have viewed Booth solely as a social reformer of the nineteenth century. They have not understood the fact that Booth's attempts at social reform came long after he had been engaged actively in the Christian ministry and relatively late in his life in that Victorian world, when he was sixty-one years old. These scholars have also failed to understand the theological pilgrimage of Booth prior to his entering into the arena of social reformation, as well as the theological foundation of his social reform.

Second, those few who have recognized some theological underpinnings of Booth's life and ministry have not completely understood that his theology evolved. They have not traced the theology of Booth from his early years to his later years, and have often written indiscriminately about some aspect of his theology, without regard for change or for the contexts in which that change was shaped.

Third, some have sensed a change of direction in Booth's thinking, but have not analyzed the change correctly. In that this third failure is the most common one in the scholarly community's dealing with Booth, it is necessary to address this more fully.

Chadwick is correct when he states that "it was true that a lot of social endeavour sprang from a desire to convert, as Booth's revivalism led him to the succour of the down-and-out."[2] Inglis in his book entitled *Churches and the Working Classes in Victorian England* expresses a similar sentiment when he contends that "the most spectacular example of a Christian converted into a social reformer by what appears to him to be the dictates of strategy"[3] was William Booth. Inglis is aware of change that took place. However, he is incorrect in his assessment of such change. He is incorrect in his statement that "It was Booth's anxiety about the Army's lack of penetrating power among slum-dwellers that turned him toward social reform."[4]

First, he is in error because there is no such trace of pessimism in Booth in the late 1880s or in 1890 concerning the Army's lack of penetrating power. The opposite is true—at this time Booth demonstrated only optimism regarding the Army's mission to the poor, although he never doubted that more could be done. Such optimism was sustained by the positive appraisal of Charles Booth regarding the work of the Army, the growing recognition and acceptance of the Army by the public, and the increase in numbers of Army officers and soldiers as the Army continued to grow outside of England.

Second, the image of Booth that Inglis goes on to portray is of a nineteenth-century social reformer. This is an incorrect and incomplete understanding of Booth, and Inglis has failed to analyze correctly the change in Booth's thinking. It is possible to define Booth by studying his theology, and his social emphasis will become apparent. It is not possible to define him strictly by his social concerns and sensitivities, even though it is this aspect of the life and ministry of Booth that is so readily present to the mind of some scholars and therefore to the general public.

Inglis and others fail to take into account the fact that his increased social awareness did not diminish Booth's earlier theological loyalties. He became a Christian who was interested in social reform, but he also remained a revivalist and evangelist. He moved from being revivalist to being revivalist and social reformer. Therein was the change for Booth. Likewise, The Salvation Army evolved from a revivalist movement to a movement that was mobilized for both revivalism and social reform, but not one without the other. It became a movement with a double mission. Therein was the change for the Army.

Third, the context of the change in Booth's theology is often missed. After The Salvation Army was named as such, Booth's primary social experience was with that Army. He became identified with the Army and the Army likewise became identified with Booth. He was, after all, the General, and, all other consideration aside, his social reality was the ongoing life and work of the Army. While his earlier theology coincided with his involvement in a revival ministry and the ministry of The Christian Mission, his later theology coincided with his involvement with the Army.

In the context of the Army's increasing redemptive mission, changes in Booth's theology evolved which both legitimated the existence of The Salvation Army and its work, and provided vision, guidance, and direction for its further work. In many ways the changes in Booth's theology provided structure for the continued redemptive work today of the Army. Booth provided the Army with a theology and with a desire consistently to act upon that theology—the waging of the salvation war on two fronts: the personal and the social.

APPENDIX

Sources for Research

There are many problems inherent in any research on William Booth. These problems stem from one crucial problem of attempting to identify the body of Booth's writings. It is evident to this researcher that William Booth wrote voluminously. Therefore, scattered literally throughout the world are private letters of Booth, and perhaps even some of his manuscripts. Due to the respect given to Booth by people in The Salvation Army, these letters and manuscripts are held in families for generations and are certainly not available to the researcher. In fact, there is no way at the present of assessing exactly how much of this primary material is "out there".

The Salvation Army has done a great job in cataloging its historical holdings at the International Heritage Center of The Salvation Army, London, England, and the Army's U.S.A. National Archives and Research Center in Alexandria, Virginia. The research for this study was conducted mainly at the U.S.A. Archives and Research Center when it was located in New York. There were two sets of materials available at the U.S.A. Archives and Research Center, and they provided the primary sources for this dissertation. Available there were many published books that William Booth wrote on a variety of subjects ranging from his doctrine of sanctification to his social scheme that he launched in 1890. This project makes use of many of those works, as will be amply shown in the endnotes and the bibliography.

Equally important, however, are the voluminous published articles that William Booth wrote mainly for Christian Mission and Salvation Army publications. Especially useful were Booth's articles contained in the following publications: *The East London Evangelist*, which was first published in October 1868 and was published until December 1869. All the issues of this publication were available at the National Archives and Research Center. This was succeeded by *The Christian Mission Magazine* which began publication in January 1870. The National Archives and Research Center held the following volumes of that publication: Volume V (1873), Volume VII (1875), Volume VIII (1876), Volume IX (1877), and Volume X (1878). *The Salvationist* succeeded The Christian Mission Magazine, and was published for only one year, from 1879 to 1880. The name of *The Salvationist* was changed in 1880 to *The War Cry*, and this is still being published by The Salvation Army. The National Archives and Research Center holdings were incomplete. They begin with Volume VII (1876), and continued with various volumes until the present. However, this study covers only until the death of William Booth in 1912, and research at the Center was concentrated on the holdings from 1876 to 1912.

Four other publications were beneficial. They were *All The World,* which The Salvation Army began publishing in November, 1884, and which were available at the National Center. The Center had also the following volumes of that publication: Volumes V-VIII (1889-1897), and Volumes XV-XIX (1899-1903); *Full Salvation,* of which the Center had only the issues from May 1892 to January 1894; and *The Conqueror* which was published from 1892 to 1897. The Center had all these volumes.

Finally, the Brown University Rockefeller Library had all the issues of a non-Salvationist magazine entitled *The Contemporary Review* for which William Booth and others interested in the work of The Salvation Army wrote occasionally. In addition to these materials, the Center had recently acquired microfilm of the minutes of The Christian Mission. These minutes provided valuable information.

The limits of available data on William Booth, therefore, become immediately obvious. The state of the evidence and the inaccessibility to other probable evidence has required me to write this study within the confines of what is available to me. This placed limits on the scope of the project, but it also provided a challenge to the scholar to continue to search for, collect, and systematize the writings of William Booth. Appropriate to that task would be the formulation of a bibliography of the writings of Booth, a task which will be imperative for the continued work on this subject. Indeed, the limits of the available data demonstrate and confirm the necessity of this study—to contribute to the scholarly world knowledge of William Booth's theology. This, in turn, may cause hitherto unknown material on William Booth to come to light.

However limited the sources at the time of the writing of this text for publication in 1989, so many opportunities arose since that time to continue my study of William Booth and his theology through a generous sabbatical program at Gordon College and several grants. Both the time and the money granted to me gave me the opportunity to continue my research at The Salvation Army's International Heritage Centre in London, England, as well as the British Library and the Lambeth Palace Library. This research has resulted in various books and articles published since the publication of this book, and constant collaboration with several scholars both inside The Salvation Army and outside of The Salvation Army that has enriched my life beyond measure. I stand in their debt.

SELECTED BIBLIOGRAPHY

Works of William Booth

Booth, William. "All Things New." *All The World* 11 January 1895): 3-7.

_____. "The Army Mother." *The War Cry* 31 (October 1910): 9.

_____. "The Atonement. Its Meaning and Importance." *The Field Officer* 16 (June 1908): 201-03.

_____. "Besetting Sins." *The War Cry* 12 (March 1891): 9.

_____. "The Chiefest Among Ten Thousand." *The Christian Mission Magazine* (November 1875): 280-83.

_____. "Christianity on Fire, No. I." *The War Cry* 13 (April 1892): 9.

_____. "Christianity on Fire, No. II." *The War Cry* 13 (May 1892): 9.

_____. "Christianity on Fire, No. III." *The War Cry* 13 (May 1892): 9.

_____. "Christianity on Fire, No. IV." *The War Cry* 13 (May 1892): 9-10

_____. "Christianity on Fire, No. V." *The War Cry* 13 (May 1892): 9.

_____. "Christianity on Fire, No. VI." *The War Cry* 13 June 1892): 9.

_____. "Christianity on Fire, No. VII." *The War Cry* 13 June1892): 9.

_____. "The Christ-Man." *Full Salvation* 9 (December 1892): 377-380.

_____. "The Coming Memorial Service at the Agricultural Hall." *The War Cry* 13 (October 1892): 9.

_____. "The Crown of Thorns." *All The World* 12 (October 1896): 433-436.

_____. "'Darkest England,' and Other Affairs." *The War Cry* 12 (January 1891): 9.

_____. *In Darkest England and the Way Out.* London: Funk and Wagnalls, 1890.

_____. "A Daughter of Ephesus, An Allegory, Chapter I." *The War Cry* 14 (August 1893): 9.

_____. "A Daughter of Ephesus, An Allegory, Chapter II." *The War Cry* 14 (August 1893): 9.

_____. "A Daughter of Ephesus, An Allegory, Chapter III." *The War Cry* 14 (August 1893): 9.

_____. "A Daughter of Ephesus, An Allegory, Chapter IV." *The War Cry* 14 (August 1893): 9.

_____. "A Daughter of Ephesus, An Allegory, Chapter V." *The War Cry* 14 (August 1893): 9.

_____. "A Daughter of Ephesus, An Allegory, Chapter VI." *The War Cry* 14 (August 1893): 9.

_____. "A Daughter of Ephesus, An Allegory, Chapter VII." *The War Cry* 14 (August 1893): 9.

_____. "Dedication." *The East London Evangelist* (October 1868): 1.

_____. *The Doctrines and Disciplines of The Salvation Army*. London: International Headquarters, 1881.

_____. *Faith Healing-A Memorandum for the Use of The Salvation Army*. London: Salvation Army, 1902.

_____. "Fight!" *All The World* 1 (May 1885): 111-113.

_____. "Forward." *The War Cry* 8 (January 1887): 9.

_____. *The Founder's Messages to Soldiers*. London: Salvationist Publishing and Supplies, 1908.

_____. "The General on the Forty-Sixth Anniversary." *The War Cry* 32 (July 1911): 9.

_____. "The General's Address," *The War Cry* 8 (January 1887): 9.

_____. "The General's Address at Exeter Hall, on Monday Evening." *The War Cry* 7 (June 1886): 9.

_____. "The General's Address at Exeter Hall, on Monday Morning, May 31st." *The War Cry* 7 (June 1886):19.

_____. "The General's Address at the Wesleyan Conference." *The War Cry* 1 (August 1880): 1.

_____. "The General's Christmas Salute." *The War Cry* 31 (December 1910):13.

_____. "The General's Greetings to the Officers, Soldiers and Friends of the British Forces of The Salvation Army." *The War Cry* 13 (February 1892): 9.

_____. "The General's Jubilee Message." *The War Cry* 15 (June 1894): 8-9.

_____. "The General's Last Appeal to Backsliders from the Ranks of The Salvation Army and to Backsliders Everywhere." *The War Cry* 13 (February 1892): 9.

_____. *The General's Letters, 1885*. London: International Headquarters, 1890.

_____. "The General's New Year Address to Officers." *The War Cry* 4 (January 10, 13, 17, 24, and February 3, 1883): 4.

_____. "The General's Opinion—Faith and Works." *The War Cry* 32 (June 1911): 8.

_____. "The General to Backsliders from the Ranks of The Salvation Army and to Backsliders Everywhere." *The War Cry* 13 (January 1892): 9-10.

_____. "Go!" *All The World* 1 (November 1884): 1-4.

_____. "God and You!" *The Christian Mission Magazine* (February 1875):34.

_____. "The Heart of True Religion." *All The World* 9 (January 1893): 1-4.

_____. "Hints to Soul Winners." *The Christian Mission Magazine* (May 1875): 124-126.

_____. "Holiness." *The War Cry* 7 (July 1886): 9.

_____. "Holiness. An Address at the Conference." *The Christian Mission Magazine* (August 1877):193-198.

_____. "Holiness. Sanctification—Objections." *The War Cry* 2 (January 1881): 1.

_____. "Holiness. Sanctification—What It Is." *The War Cry* 2 (April 1881): 1.

_____. *How to Be Saved*. London: Salvationist Publishing and Supplies, n.d.

___. "How to Conquer." *The Conqueror* 4 (July 1895): 299.

___. "How to Go Ahead!" *The War Cry* 7 (May 1886): 9.

___. "How to Retain Entire Sanctification." *The Christian Mission Magazine* (January 1873): 6-7.

___. "How to Retain Entire Sanctification." *The Christian Mission Magazine* (February 1873): 22-23.

___. "The Imitation of Jesus Christ, No. I." *The War Cry* 14 (September 1893): 9.

___. "The Imitation of Jesus Christ, No. II." *The War Cry* 14 (September 1893): 8-9.

___. "The Imitation of Jesus Christ, No. III." *The War Cry* 14 (October 1893): 1-2.

___. "The Imitation of Jesus Christ, No. IV." *The War Cry* 14 (October 1893): 9.

___. *International Congress Addresses*, 1904. London: Salvation Army Book Department, 1904.

___. *International Social Council Addresses*, 1911. London: Salvation Army Printing Works, 1912.

___. *International Staff Council Addresses*, 1904. London: Salvation Army Book Department, 1904.

___. "An Interview with His Late Majesty King Edward VII." *The War Cry* 31 (May 1910): 9-10.

___. *A Ladder to Holiness*. London: Salvationist Publishing and Supplies, 1926.

___. "Letter from the General to Backsliders from the Ranks of The Salvation Army." *The War Cry* 13 (January 1892):9.

___. "Letter from William Booth to the Brethren and Sisters Labouring for Jesus in Connection with the Dunedin Hall Christian Mission, Edinburgh." *The East London Evangelist* (April 1869): 103-105.

___. "Letters from The General to the Soldiers of The Salvation Army. More About Women's Rights." *The Field Officer* 9 (November 1901):513-514.

___. "The Majors' Councils. Notes of The General's Address." *The War Cry* 3 (November 1882):3.

___. "Memorable Challenge!" *The War Cry* 32 (May 1911):9.

___. "A Message from the General." *The War Cry* 33 (June 1912):9.

___. "The Millennium; or, The Ultimate Triumph of Salvation Army Principles." *All The World* 6 (August 1890):337-343.

___. "The Mind of Christ." Full Salvation 11 (January 1894):3-6.

___. "My Idea of the Millennium." *Review of Reviews* 2 (July/December 1890):130.

___. "On Salvation Women." *The Field Officer* 9 (September 1901):422-424.

___. *Orders and Regulations for Field Officers of The Salvation Army*. London: Salvation Army, 1888.

___. "Our New Name." *The Salvationist* (January 1879): 1-3.

___. "Our War Congress." *The Christian Mission Magazine* (September 1878):225-227.

___. "A Passion for Souls." *The Conqueror* I (October 1892):273-275.

_____. "The Past of the War." *The Christian Mission Magazine* (September 1878):236-245.

_____. "Preface." *All The World* 1 (November 1884): 1-4.

_____. "Preface" to *The New Testament Commentary*, Salvation Army Edition. London: Salvation Army Publishing Department, n.d.

_____. *Purity of Heart*. London: Salvation Army Book Room, 1902.

_____. *Religion for Every Day*. London: Salvationist Publishing and Supplies, n.d.

_____. "Revelation of God." *The War Cry* 32 (April 19II):2.

_____. "Rise and Fall." *The Christian Mission Magazine* (January 1878):1-4.

_____. "Rushing into War." *The Christian Mission Magazine* (May 1878): 113-116.

_____. "The Salvation Army." *The Salvationist* (February 1879): 29-33.

_____. comp. *The Salvation Army Songs*. London: Salvationist Publishing and Supplies, n.d.

_____. "Salvation for Both Worlds." *All The World* 5 January 1889):1-6.

_____. comp. *The Salvation Soldiers' Song Book*. Toronto: Salvation Army Publishing House, n.d.

_____. *Salvation Soldiery*. London: Partridge and Company, 1883.

_____. *The Seven Spirits; or, What I Teach My Officers*. London: Salvation Army Book Department, 1907.

_____. "Some of the Things I Want to See in 1912." *The War Cry* 32 (December 1911):9.

_____. *Talks with Officers of The Salvation Army*. London: Salvation Army, 1921.

_____. *To My Officers: A Letter from the General on His Eightieth Birthday*. St. Albans: Salvation Army Printing works, 1909.

_____. "To My Officers Throughout the World." *The Officer* 1 January 1893):1-3.

_____. "To My Officers Throughout the World." *The Officer* 8 June 1900):201-202,.

_____. "To the Officers and Soldiers of The Salvation Army." *The Salvationist* (October 1879):253-256.

_____. "Universal Peace. A Christmas Address." *The War Cry* 2 (December 1881):4.

_____. *Visions*. London: Salvation Army Book Department, 1906.

_____. "What Are You Going to Do in 1869?" *The East London Evangelist* (January 1869):49-52.

_____. "What is the General Puzzled About?" *The War Cry* 7 (March 1886):9.

_____. "What is the Salvation Army?" *The Contemporary Review* 41 (August 1882): 175-182.

_____. "What is The Salvation Army?" *The War Cry* 33 (July 1912):2.

_____. "Will You Let Me In?" *The War Cry* 33 (May 1912):2.

_____. "Worldliness." *The Officer* 7 (January 1899):10-14.

Works of Catherine Booth

Booth, Catherine. "Do Something!" *The Salvation News* (July 1880): 1-2.

___. "Filled With The Spirit." *The War Cry* 1 (August 1880): 1.

___. "Filled With The Spirit (Concluded)." *The War Cry* 1 (August 1880): 1.

___. *The Highway of Our God.* London: Salvationist Publishing and Supplies, n.d.

___. "The Holy Ghost." *All The World* 16 (June 1900):339-342.

___. "The Kingdom of Christ." *All The World* 1 (August 1885): 183-184.

___. "The Kingdom of Christ." *All The World* 1 (September 1885):207-209.

___. *Life and Death.* London: International Headquarters, 1890.

___. "Our Commission." *All The World* 1 (April 1885):83-85.

___. *Papers on Aggressive Christianity.* London: International Headquarters, 1891.

___. *Popular Christianity.* London: Salvation Army Book Depot, 1887.

___. *The Salvation Army in Relation to the Church and State, and Other Addresses.* London: International Headquarters, 1889.

Works of Bramwell Booth

Booth, Bramwell. *Aspects of Social Work in The Salvation Army.* London: Salvation Army Book Department, 1917.

___. *Echoes and Memories.* New York: George H. Doran Company, 1925.

___. "The General." *The War Cry* 33 (September 1912):2.

___. "The Salvation Army." *Encyclopedia of Religion and Ethics.* Edited by James Hastings, 12 vols. New York: Charles Scribner's Sons, 1921. 11:151-160.

___. *Servants of All.* London: Salvationist Publishing and Supplies, 1900.

___. *Social Reparation, or Personal Impressions of Work for Darkest England.* London: International Headquarters, 1899.

___. *The Why and Wherefore of The Salvation Army Orders and Regulations.* London: Salvationist Publishing and Supplies, 1922.

Works of Other Members of the Booth Family

Booth, Ballington. "A Jubilee Glimpse of the General." *The Conqueror* 3 (July 1894):258-259.

Booth, Evangeline. *Toward a Better World.* Garden City, New York: Doubleday, Doran and Company, 1928.

Booth, Herbert, and Booth, Corry. *Songs of Peace and War.* London: Salvation Army Printing and Publishing Department, 1890.

Booth-Clibborn, Arthur. "The Pentecostal Programme." *All The World* 11 (June 1895):401-405.

Booth-Tucker, Frederick de Latour. *The Life of Catherine Booth*, 2 vols. New York: Fleming H. Revell Company, 1892.

Bramwell-Booth, Catherine. *Bramwell Booth.* London: Rich and Cowan, 1933.

___. *Catherine Booth.* London: Hodder and Stoughton, 1970.

Works on William Booth and The Salvation Army

"An American Review of Darkest England." *Review of Reviews* 4 (July/December 1891):390.

"As It Was in the Beginning!" *All the World* 17 (July 1901):339-342.

Ausubel, Herman. "General Booth's Scheme of Social Salvation." *American Historical Review* 56 (April 1951):519-525.

Avery, Gordon. *Companion to the Song Book of The Salvation Army.* London: Salvationist Publishing and Supplies, 1961.

Bateman, Charles T. *Life of General Booth.* New York: Association Press, 1912.

Begbie, Harold. "Booth, William." *Dictionary of National Biography* 1912-1921). London: Oxford University Press, 1921.

____. *The Life of General William Booth.* 2 vols. New York: The Macmillan Company, 1920.

____. "The Soul of the General." *The War Cry* 33 (May 1912):8,11.

Cadman, Elijah. "The New Kingdom." *All The World* 11 July 1895): 1-4.

Chesham, Howard, and Chesham, Sallie. *Combat Songs of The Salvation Army.* New York: Salvationist Publishing and Supplies, 1976.

Coates, Thomas F. G. *The Prophet of the Poor.* New York: E. P. Dutton and Company, 1906.

Cobbe, Frances Power. "The Last Revival." *The Contemporary Review* 41 (August 1882): 182-189.

"The Conquest of the World." *All The World* 17 (February 1901): 56-61.

"The Conversion of the World." *The East London Evangelist* (October 1869): 199-200.

Coutts, Frederick. *Bread for My Neighbour.* London: Hodder and Stoughton, 1978.

____. *No Discharge in This War.* London: Hodder and Stoughton, 1974.

Coutts, John. *The Salvationists.* London: A. R. Mowbray and Company, Ltd., 1978.

Cox, Fred. "The Founder." Special Lecture to Cadets by Brigadier Fred Cox, the Founder's secretary, on January 4, 1924.

Davidson, Randall T. "The Methods of The Salvation Army." *The Contemporary Review* 41 (August 1882):189-199.

"Dr. Adam Clarke and the General's Spiritual Father." *The Conqueror* 5 (July 1896):306.

Duff, Mildred. "Our First General and the Place He Gave to Women." *The Field Officer* 20 (October 1912):373-376.

Eason, Andrew Mark. *Women in God's Army: Gender and Equality in the Early Salvation Army* (Waterloo, Ontario, Canada: Wilfrid Laurier University Press, 2003).

Eason, Andrew M. and Roger J. Green. *Boundless Salvation: The Shorter Writings of William Booth.* New York: Peter Lang, 2012.

England, M. "The Salvation Army." In *London in the Nineteenth Century*, pp. 277-304. Edited by Sir Walter Besant. London: Adam and Charles Black, 1909.

Ervine, St. John. *God's Soldier: General William Booth*. 2 vols. New York: The Macmillan Company, 1935.

Farrar, Dean. "Social Amelioration." *The War Cry* 32 (May 1911):2.

"Festival of Thanksgiving." *The War Cry* 33 (May 1912):9-10.

"Fifty Years' Salvation Service: Some of Its Lessons and Results. Interview with the General." *All The World* 10 (July 1894): 1-9.

"The General and His Religion." *The War Cry* 33 (May 1912):2.

"The General and Mr. Winston Churchill." *The War Cry* 31 (October 1910):8.

"The General's Jubilee. The General Interviewed." *The War Cry* 15 (April 1894):9.

"The General's Jubilee. An Interview with the General." *The War Cry* 15 (March 1894):9.

Grant, Donaldson. "General William Booth." *All The World* 19 (March 1903):115-119.

Green, Roger J. *Catherine Booth: A Biography of the Cofounder of The Salvation Army*. Grand Rapids, MI: Baker Books, 1996.

Green, Roger J. *The Life & Ministry of William Booth: Founder of The Salvation Army*. Nashville, TN: Abingdon Press, 2005.

Greenwood, H. *General Booth and His Critics*. London: Howe and Company, 1891.

"Higher Criticism." *All The World* 13 (August 1897):338-340.

Hollins, John. "The Salvation Army: A Note of Warning." *The Contemporary Review* 74 (September 1898):436-445.

Horridge, Glenn. *The Salvation Army: Origins and Early Days: 1865-1900*. Godalming, Surrey, England: Ammonite Books, 1993.

"In Darkest England: Progress Along the Way Out." *Review of Reviews* 3 (January-June 1891): 160-161.

Lawley, John. "Down with the Gates!" *The War Cry* 14 (October 1893):12.

___. "Down with the Gates!" *The War Cry* 14 (November 1893):12.

Loch, C. S., Bosanquet, Bernard, and Dwyer, Philip. *Criticisms on "General" Booth's Social Scheme*. London: Swan Sonnenschein and Company,1891.

McKinley, Edward. *Marching to Glory*. New York: Harper and Row, Publishers, 1980.

Magnuson, Norris. *Salvation in the Slums: Evangelical Social Work, 1865-1920*. The American Theological Library Association Monograph Series, No. 10. Metuchen, New Jersey: Scarecrow Press, 1977.

Manning, Henry Edward. "The Salvation Army." *The Contemporary Review* 41 (August 1882):335-342.

Massingham, Hugh. *The Great Victorians*. London: Ivor Nicholson and Watson, n.d.

"Minutes of the First Conference of The Christian Mission." New York: The Salvation Army Archives and Research Center, MS 38, n.d.

"Minutes of The Christian Mission, 1876."

Merritt, John G. *Historical Dictionary of The Salvation Army*. Lanham, MD.: The Scarecrow Press, Inc., 2006.

Needham, Philip D. "Redemption and Social Reformation: A Theological Study of William Booth and His Movement." M.Th. thesis, Princeton Theological Seminary, 1967.

Nicol, Alex M. *General Booth and The Salvation Army*. London: Herbert and Daniel, 1911.

"Our View of the Bible." *The War Cry* 4 (March 1883):4.

J. H. P. " 'Thy Kingdom Come'—Amen." *All The World* 1 (February 1885):37-39.

Page, Jesse. *General Booth: The Man and His Work*. London: S. W. Partridge, 1901.

Peek, Francis. "General Booth's Social Work." *The Contemporary Review* 62 (July 1892):59-84.

___. "In Darkest England and the Way Out." *The Contemporary Review* 58 (December 1890):796-807.

Railton, George Scott. *The Authoritative Life of General William Booth*. New York: The Reliance Trading Company, 1912.

___. *Heathen England*. London: International Headquarters, 1891.

___. *Twenty-One Years Salvation Army*. London: Salvation Army Publishing Offices, 1887.

Rightmire, R. David. *Sacraments and The Salvation Army: Pneumatological Foundations* (Metuchen, NJ: The Scarecrow Press, Inc., 1990).

Robertson, Roland. "The Salvation Army: The Persistence of Sectarianism." in *Patterns of Sectarianism*, pp. 49-105. Edited by Brian R. Wilson. London: Heinemann Educational Books, 1967.

Salvation Army Ceremonies. London: Salvationist Publishing and Supplies, 1966.

Sandall, Robert. *The History of The Salvation Army*. 8 vols. London: Thomas Nelson and Sons, 1947-1966. Vols. 1-3 by Robert Sandall, vols. 4-5 by Arch Wiggins, vols. 6-7 by Frederick Coutts (London: Hodder and Stoughton), vol. 8 by Henry Gariepy (Grand Rapids, MI: William B. Eerdmans Publishing Co., 2000).

"A Second-Coming Meeting at the Congress Hall, Clapton." *The War Cry* 7 (May 1886): 11.

Smith, J. Evan. *Booth the Beloved*. London: Oxford University Press, 1949.

Stead, W. T. "The Book of the Year-In Darkest England." *Review of Reviews* 2 (July-December 1890):651-656.

___. "The Darkest England Scheme." *Review of Reviews* 3 (January-June 1891): 14-17.

___. *General Booth, A Biographical Sketch*. London: Isbister and Company, 1891.

___. "In Darkest England and the Way Out." Review of Reviews 2 (July-December 1890):492-507.

Steele, Harold C. *I Was a Stranger*. New York: Exposition Press, 1954.

Telford, John. "An English Apostle. Life of William Booth, the Founder of The Salvation Army." *London Quarterly and Holborn Review* 19 (1920):237-249.

Watson, Bernard. *Soldier Saint*. London: Hodder and Stoughton, 1970.

Waldron, John D. *Creed and Deed: Toward a Christian Theology of Social Services in The Salvation Army* (Toronto, Canada: The Salvation Army, 1986).

"What We Believe. The Inspiration of the Bible." *The Field Officer* 13 (June 1905):221-223.

"What We Believe. The Inspiration of the Bible." *The Field Officer* 13 (July 1905):257-258.

Wilson, Bryan. *Religious Sects: A Sociological Study*. New York: McGraw-Hill Book Company, 1970.

Other Works

Altholz, Josef L. *The Churches in the Nineteenth Century*. New York: the Bobbs-Merrill Company, 1967.

Armytage, W. H. G. *Heavens Below*. London: Routledge and Kegan Paul, 1961.

Barnett, Samuel A. "Twenty-Five Years of East London." *The Contemporary Review* 74 (August 1898):280-289.

Besant, Walter. *East London*. New York: The Century Company, 1901.

Besant, Walter, ed. *London in the Nineteenth Century*. London: Adam and Charles Black, 1909.

Bloesch, Donald G. *The Evangelical Renaissance*. Grand Rapids, Michigan: William B. Eerdmans Publishing Company, 1973.

Booth, Charles. *Life and Labour of the People in London*. 17 vols. London: MacMillan Company, Ltd., 1902.

____ . *On the City: Physical Pattern and Social Structure*. Chicago: University of Chicago Press, 1967.

Briggs, Asa. *Victorian Cities*. New York: Harper and Row, Publishers, 1963.

Chadwick, Owen. *The Victorian Church*. 2 vols. London: Adam and Charles Black, 1966.

Clark, G. Kitson. *The Making of Victorian England*. Cambridge, Massachusetts: Harvard University Press, 1962.

Clark, Henry W. *History of English Nonconformity*. 2 vols. London: Chapman and Hull, 1913.

Davies, Rupert E. *Methodism*. Harmondsworth, Middlesex, England: Penguin Books, 1963.

Dayton, Donald. *Discovering an Evangelical Heritage*. New York: Harper and Row, Publishers, 1976.

Dyos, H. J. and Michael Wolff, eds. *The Victorian City*. 2 vols. London: Routledge and Kegan Paul, 1973.

Elliott-Binns, L. E. *The Development of English Theology in the Later Nineteenth Century*. London: Longmans, Green, and Company, 1952.

____ . *Religion in the Victorian Era*. London: The Lutterworth Press, 1936.

Field, Benjamin. *The Student's Handbook of Christian Theology*. Edited by John C. Symans. Introduction by L. Tyerman. New York: Methodist Book Concern, 1886.

Halevey, Elie. *A History of the English People* (Translated by E. I. Watkin) London: Ernest Benn, Ltd., 1929.

Heasman, Kathleen. *Evangelicals in Action*. London: Geoffrey Bles, 1962.

"Holiness. Extracts from James Caughey." *The War Cry* 1 (March 1880): 1-2.

Houghton, Walter E. *The Victorian Frame of Mind*, 1830-1870. New Haven: Yale University Press, 1957.

Huxley, Thomas H. *Evolution and Ethics*. 9 vols. New York: D. Appleton and Company, 1894.

____ . *Social Diseases and Worse Remedies*. London: MacMillan and Company, 1891.

Inglis, K. S. *Churches and the Working Classes in Victorian England*. Toronto: University of Toronto Press, 1963.

McLoughlin, William G. *Modem Revivalism*. New York: The Ronald Press Company, 1959.

Reardon, B. M. G. *Religious Thought in the Nineteenth Century*. Cambridge: The University Press, 1966.

Sandeen, Ernest R. *The Roots of Fundamentalism*. Chicago: The University of Chicago Press, 1970.

____ . "Toward a Historical Interpretation of the Origins of Fundamentalism." *Church History* 36 (1967):66-83.

Shepperson, George. "The Comparative Study of Millenarian Movements." In *Millennial Dreams in Action*, pp. 44-52. Edited by Sylvia L. Thrupp. The Hague: Mouton, 1962.

Smith, Timothy L. *Revivalism and Social Reform*. New York: Abingdon Press, 1957.

Sugden, Edward H., ed. *Wesley's Standard Sermons*. 2 vols. London: The Epworth Press, 1966.

Trevelyan, G. M. *English Social History*. New York: David McKay Company, 1965.

____ . *History of England*, Vol. III, Garden City, New York: Doubleday and Company, Inc., 1952.

Troeltsch, Ernst. *The Social Teaching of the Christian Churches*. 2 vols. New York: Harper and Row, Publishers, 1960.

Weber, Max. *The Protestant Ethic and the Spirit of Capitalism*. New York: Charles Scribner's Sons, 1958.

____ . "The Protestant Sects and the Spirit of Capitalism," In *From Max Weber: Essays in Sociology*, pp. 302-322. Edited by Hans H. Gerth and C. Wright Mills. New York: Oxford University Press, 1974.

NOTES TO THE CHAPTERS

Introduction

The Victorian England of William Booth

1. G. M. Trevelyan, *History of England*, 3 vols. (Garden City, New York: Doubleday and Company, Inc., 1952), 3:138.
2. G. M. Trevelyan, *English Social History* (New York: David McKay Company, Inc., 1965), p. 535.
3. Walter Besant, *East London* (New York: The Century Company, 1901), p.8.
4. Ibid.
5. Trevelyan, *English Social History*, p. 464.
6. Owen Chadwick, *The Victorian Church*, 2 vols. (London: Adam and Charles Black, 1966) 1:325. In a later reference Chadwick noted that "Few dissenting congregations could survive as independent communities in a slum, for the money of the working poor could pay neither the rent of the chapel nor the stipend of the minister" (Ibid., 1:329).
7. Trevelyan, *History of England*, pp. 140-141.
8. Elie Halevy, *A History of the English People*, 3 vols. Translated by E. I. Watkin (London: Ernest Benn Limited, 1929),3:166.
9. Walter Besant, ed., *London in the Nineteenth Century* (London: Adam and Charles Black, 1909), p. 274. See also Samuel A. Barnett, "Twenty-Five Years of East London," *The Contemporary Review* 74 (August 1898):280-289.
10. Chadwick, *The Victorian Church*, 1:1.
11. Ibid., 1:5.
12. Ibid.
13. Trevelyan, *History of England*, 3: 131.
14. There are many biographies on the life of William Booth. Some of them are: Charles T. Bateman, *Life of General Booth* (New York: Association Press, 1912); Harold Begbie, *The Life of General William Booth*, 2 vols. (New York: The Macmillan Company, 1920); Frederick de Latour Booth-Tucker, *William Booth, The General of The Salvation Army* (New York: The Salvation Army Printing and Publishing House, 1898); Thomas F. Coates, *The Prophet of the Poor* (London: Hodder and Stoughton, 1905); St. John Ervine, *God's Soldier:*

General William Booth, 2 vols. (New York: The Macmillan Company, 1935); Alex M. Nichol, *General Booth and The Salvation Army* (London: Herbert and Daniel, 1911); G. S. Railton, *The Authoritative Life of General William Booth* (New York: The Reliance Trading Company, 1912); J. Evan Smith, *Booth the Beloved* (London: Oxford University Press, 1949); W. T. Stead, *General Booth* (London: Isbister and Company, 1891); Harold C. Steele, *I Was A Stranger* (New York: Exposition Press, 1954). Since the publication of this book there have been other biographies written, including my biography entitled *The Life and Ministry of William Booth: Founder of The Salvation Army* (Nashville, TN: Abingdon Press, 2005).

The best complete history of The Salvation Army during Booth's lifetime is entitled *The History of The Salvation Army*, 8 vols. Vols. 1-3 by Robert Sandall; vols. 4-5 by Arch R. Wiggins (London: Thomas Nelson); vols. 6-7 by Frederick Coutts (London: Hodder and Stoughton); vol. 8 by Henry Gariepy (Grand Rapids, MI: William B. Eerdmans Publishing Company, 2000).

Two shorter, but excellent, volumes on the history of The Salvation Army are Frederick Coutts, *No Discharge in This War* (London: Hodder and Stoughton, 1974), and Frederick Coutts, *Bread For My Neighbour* (London: Hodder and Stoughton, 1978). Two fine books which deal with religious life in Victorian England treat the Army extensively, and provide excellent sources on The Salvation Army during Booth's lifetime. They are K. S. Inglis, *Churches and the Working Classes in Victorian England* (Toronto: University of Toronto Press, 1963), chap. 5, and Owen Chadwick, *The Victorian Church*, 2 vols. (London: Adam and Charles Black, 1966), vol. 2, chap. 5.

The Salvation Army was organized from The Christian Mission on a military basis in 1878, and the official title of The Salvation Army was incorporated in 1880. Military language became an integral part of the organization, so, for example, the churches were called corps, the groups that were in the process of becoming churches were called outposts, and death was referred to as being promoted to Glory. The organizational structure took the form of officers (ministers) and soldiers (laypersons). Officers took the titles of rank, such as General (of which there is only one at a time), Commissioners, Colonels, Majors, Captains, and Lieutenants. Of this organization one wrote: "What was inconsistent with true soldiership for Christ was as rapidly as possible got rid of, and all that was useful in the teachings of the earth's armies was carefully learnt. Part No. 1 of *Orders and Regulations for The Salvation Army* was published in 1878, after long and careful study of the manuals of the British Army" (George Railton, *Heathen England* [London: International headquarters, 1891], (p. 29). See also Bramwell Booth, *The Why and Wherefore of The Salvation Army Orders and Regulations* (London: Salvationist Publishing and Supplies, 1922), pp. 62-63.

15. See Stead, *General Booth*, p. 84.

16. In the 1840s James Caughey preached in England, and William Booth heard him. Philip D. Needham, speaking of the influence of that evangelist upon William Booth, states that "he learned much from this man that was to be of both theological and practical value in his future work among poor and simple people" (Philip D. Needham, "Redemption and Social Reformation: A Theological Study of William Booth and His Movement" [M. Th. thesis, Princeton Theological Seminary, 1967]. p. 59). See also pp. 106-109; Begbie, *The Life of General William Booth*, 1:9, 61-62, 163, 284; Ervine, *God's Soldier: General William Booth*, 1:37, 74.

The primary influence of James Caughey upon William Booth was in Caughey's teaching of the Wesleyan doctrine of holiness and the work of the Holy Spirit in the lives of believers. This is clear in an article in a Salvation Army publication entitled *The Conqueror* and published in July 1896. The article incorrectly begins, "In view of the fact that the General was converted under the preaching of the late Rev. James Caughey, the following passage from the pen of this renowned evangelist becomes of almost historical interest" ("Dr. Adam Clarke and the General's Spiritual Father," *The Conqueror* 5 July 1896]: 306). Booth was converted two years before first hearing Caughey. See also Chadwick, *The Victorian Church*, 1 :379, and "Holiness. Extracts from James Caughey," *The War Cry* 1 (March 1880), 1-2.

17. Quoted in Begbie, *The Life of General William Booth*, 1 :367-368.
18. Frederick de Lautour Booth-Tucker, *The Life of Catherine Booth*, 2 vols. (New York: Fleming H. Revell Company, 1892). 1:74.
19. Stead, *General Booth*, pp. 87-88.
20. Quoted in Begbie, *The Life of General William Booth*, 1 :367-368.
21. Quoted in Wiggins, *The History of The Salvation Army*, 4:219.
22. Trevelyan, *English Social History*, p. 569. See also Stead, *General Booth*, p. 13. Stead wrote that "The Salvation Army represents, in the General's theory, what Wesleyanism would have come to if it had not ceased to develop when its founder died." See also Begbie, *The Life of General William Booth*, 1:7,281.
23. Chadwick, *The Victorian Church*, 1 :6.
24. For an example of this see William Booth, "Christianity on Fire, No. VII," *The War Cry* 18 June 1892):9; William Booth, "The Imitation of Jesus Christ, Part II," *The War Cry* 21 (September 1893):8; William Booth, "Memorable Challenge," *The War Cry* 56 (May 1911):9; William Booth, *Religion for Every Day* (London: Salvationist Publishing and Supplies, n.d.), p. 143. As has been noted, William Booth was sometimes compared to John Wesley, and there is one reference where he was compared to Martin Luther. See "Festival of Thanksgiving," *The War Cry* 58 (May 1912):9. The writer of that article wrote that seeing Booth "reminded us of another champion of the truth who, in widely differing surroundings, has declared, 'Here I stand, I can do no other.' "

25. For an example of this see William Booth, *Religion for Every Day*, pp. 133-134.

26. For an example of this see ibid., p. 65.

27. For examples of this see William Booth, *In Darkest England and the Way Out* (London: Funk and Wagnalls, 1890), pp. 45, 64.

28. For examples of this see William Booth, "Letter from William Booth to the Brethren and Sisters Labouring for Jesus in Connection with the Dunedin Hall Christian Mission, Edinburgh," *The East London Evangelist* (April 1869):104; William Booth, "Holiness. An Address at the Conference," *The Christian Mission Magazine* (August 1877):197; William Booth, "Rise and Fall," *The Christian Mission Magazine* January 1878):3; William Booth, "Christianity on Fire, No. V," *The War Cry* 18 (May 1892):9; William Booth, "The Imitation of Jesus Christ, No. I," *The War Cry* 21 (September 1893):9; William Booth, *Purity of Heart* (London: The Salvation Army Book-Room, 1902), pp. 25-26; William Booth, *Religion For Every Day*, pp. 16-17, 31-33,42,53,146,149.

29. William Booth, *In Darkest England and the Way Out*, p. 280.

30. William Booth, "The Crown of Thorns," *All The World* 17 (October 1896):436. See also William Booth, "Christianity on Fire, No. VI," *The War Cry* 18 June 1892):9.

31. William Booth, *In Darkest England and the Way Out*, pp. xxx-xxxi. For other examples of this see ibid., pp. 21,47,86,125; William Booth, *Purity of Heart*, p. 102.

32. For examples of this see William Booth, "A Daughter of Ephesus, An Allegory, Chapter VI," *The War Cry* 21 (August 1893):9; "Fifty Years' Salvation Service: Some of Its Lessons and Results. Interview with the General," *All The World* 14 July 1894):6; William Booth, *Purity of Heart*, pp. 6, 14,26-27,38,47,66-67,73,92,95; William Booth, "Memorable Challenge!" p. 9; William Booth, *Religion For Every Day*, p. 151; William Booth, *A Ladder to Holiness* (London: Salvationist Publishing and Supplies, 1926), p. 5.

33. William Booth, "A Daughter of Ephesus, An Allegory, Chapter III," *The War Cry* 21 (August 1893):9; William Booth, "A Daughter of Ephesus, An Allegory, Chapter VI," p. 9.

34. William Booth, *Religion For Every Day*, p. 93.

35. William Booth, *Purity of Heart*, p. 35.

36. Ibid., p. 90.

37. Ibid., p. 39.

38. William Booth wrote four songs. Many of the members of his family, as well as many people who were influential in The Christian Mission and The Salvation Army, wrote songs also. See William Booth, comp., *The Salvation Army Songs* (London: The Salvationist Publishing and Supplies, n.d.). See also Gordon Avery, *Companion to the Song Book of The Salvation Army* (London: Salvationist Publishing and Supplies, 1961).

39. William Booth, "Hints to Soul Winners," *The Christian Mission Magazine* (May 1875):125.
40. William Booth, *In Darkest England and the Way Out*, p. 158.
41. Ibid., see also pp. 129, 159.

CHAPTER I

STAGE ONE: THE MINISTRY AND THEOLOGY
OF WILLIAM BOOTH TO 1878

1. William Booth, "Salvation for Both Worlds," *All the World* 5 January 1889): 1.
2. Chadwick, *The Victorian Church*, 2:289.
3. *The Christian Mission Magazine* July 1875):191.
4. *The Christian Mission Magazine* January 1876): 18-19.
5. Chadwick, *The Victorian Church*, 2:471.
6. Quoted in Begbie, *The Life of General William Booth*, 1 :367. See also 1 :207.
7. Quoted in ibid., 1:328. See also 1:351; William Booth, "What is the General Puzzled About?" *The War Cry* 7 (March 1886):9; William Booth, "The General's Address at Exeter Hall on Monday Evening," *The War Cry* 7 June 1886):9; "Higher Criticism," *All The World* 18 (August 1897):339-340; Donaldson Grant, "General William Booth," *All The World* 24 (March 1903):119.
8. Quoted in Sandall, *The History of The Salvation Army*, 1 :93.
9. William Booth, *Religion for Every Day*, p. 159.
10. Ibid., pp. 159-160. See also William Booth, "Our New Name," *The Salvationist* January 1879):1; "Fifty Years' Salvation Service: Some of Its Lessons and Results. Interview with The General," pp. 3-4; Begbie, *The Life of General William Booth*, 2: 176; Wiggins, *The History of The Salvation Army*, 4:255; Edward McKinley, *Marching to Glory* (New York: Harper and Row, 1980), p. 33.
11. William Booth, *A Ladder to Holiness*, p. 4. This quotation provides a typical rehearsal by William Booth of the two greatest influences upon his own life and faith: the influence of the Bible as the source of revelation, and the influence of his own practical experiences through relationships with his "comrades" and events in his own life that confirmed what he had learned from Scripture and assisted him in formulating judgments about proper Christian conduct. However, his reference to "the light God has given me by His Holy Spirit in my own heart" does not constitute a separate source of authority for Booth, some kind of personalized and privatized inner voice, Quaker style, apart from the Bible or apart from his own experiences in life. The language may be taken generally in relationship to the Bible and to an understanding of the Bible. The Holy Spirit assisted Booth in comprehending the revelation from God in Scriptures. This illumination by the Holy Spirit

was an important function of the Holy Spirit for every believer. This was the witness of the Spirit. In *The Doctrines and Disciplines of The Salvation Army* for 1880, Section 25 on the Bible, this was explained in the following way: in answer to the question "How am I—a Salvationist Soldier—to make the best use of my Bible?" came the following instruction— "Depend on the Holy Spirit to reveal the real meaning to your soul" (Quoted in "Our View of the Bible," *The War Cry* 4 [March 1883]:4).

12. William Booth, "What is The Salvation Army?" *The Contemporary Review* 41 (August 1882):176.
13. Ibid.
14. Chadwick, *The Victorian Church*, 1 :466-467.
15. Ibid., p. 468.
16. Ibid.
17. Ibid.
18. Ibid., p. 372.
19. Ibid., p. 4.
20. William Booth, "Dedication," *The East London Evangelist* (October 1868): 1. This spirit of toleration was not some abstract concept that William Booth was not able to put into practice in his own ministry or in the ministries of The Christian Mission or The Salvation Army. His sense of toleration demonstrated itself in very practical ways. Among his admonitions to workers of The Christian Mission regarding the street services that they held, Booth warned, "Never mention deprecatingly any other religious body" (Quoted in Begbie, *The Life of General William Booth*, 1:370). In negotiations with the Church of England from 1882 to 1883 as to whether The Salvation Army would consider becoming part of that Church, William Booth was most congenial with the appointed representatives, and one of his biographers correctly observed that "it was not his business to quarrel with the churches, and he had a natural detestation of controversy" (Ibid., 2:24).

Catherine Booth shared this spirit of toleration. She, like William Booth, believed that God had ordained The Christian Mission and The Salvation Army to a special work, and she was most happy to invite anyone to share in that work of redemption. However, that work must not be done at the expense of, or the deprecation of, other groups or other denominations. Catherine Booth clarified this attitude of toleration in a book that was published in 1883 entitled *The Salvation Army in Relation to the Church and State.* There she wrote the following: "It is one of our most emphatic instructions to our officers: 'It is not your business to find fault with other people. Rejoice in all the good done, by whomsoever it is done.' We have acted on this ourselves from the beginning .... Neither are we diverse from the churches in the great fundamental doctrines of Christianity. We have not adopted any of the new gospels of the times. We have not given up any of the fundamental doctrines of Christianity, such as the Fall, the universal call to Repentance, Justification by faith through Jesus Christ, a life of obedience, Heaven and Hell." (Catherine Booth, *The Salvation Army in Relation to Church and State* [London: International Headquarters, 1889J, pp. 28-30). See also William Booth, *In Darkest England and the Way Out*, pp. 110, 139; Donaldson Grant, "General William Booth," pp. 117-118; William Booth, "An Interview with His Late Majesty King Edward VII," *The War Cry* 54 (May 1910): 10; Sandall, *The History of The Salvation Army*, 2:324. In the latter reference Sandall noted that a publication entitled *Purpose and Character of Salvation Army Literature* included a warning by William Booth that Army literature must make "no unfavorable reflections on Christian churches."

21. Minutes of the First Conference of The Christian Mission, 1870 (London: Salvationist Publishing and Supplies, MS 38, 1982), p. 15.

22. Ibid., p. 16.

23. Ibid.

24. Chadwick, *The Victorian Church*, 1 :469.

25. Ibid., p. 468.

26. William Booth, "What Are You Going to Do in 1869?" *The East London Evangelist* January 1869):51. In his book entitled *How to Be Saved* Booth set forth his understanding of the work of Christ for the individual who believes. He stated that "I am sure that He will not reject me. Nay, as well as I can, I believe that He does at this very moment take me in. He forgives me now. His precious Blood washed all my sins away. He was wounded for my transgressions; He was bruised for my iniquities; the punishment I ought to have endured was laid upon Him, and with His sufferings I am healed" (William Booth, *How to Be Saved* [London: Salvationist Publishing and Supplies, n.d., p. 6). This affirmation of personal salvation from sin was also part of the theology of Catherine Booth. She referred to it when she stated that "we take it to be fundamental that if the soul is not right, the service cannot be right, and therefore make the soul the first and chief care" (Quoted in Wiggins, *The History of the Salvation Army*, 4:385).

27. Quoted in Begbie, *The Life of General William Booth*, 1: 149.

28. Minutes of the First Conference of The Christian Mission, 1870, pp. 16-17.

29. Ibid., p. 16. There is an interesting scribal error made in the writing of these minutes. The person wrote: "We believe that our first parents were created in a state of infancy ... ." Fortunately, the word "infancy" was crossed out, and the correct word "innocence" was placed in the margin of the manuscript.

30. Begbie, *The Life of General William Booth*, 1 :24.

31. "Fifty Years' Salvation Service: Some of Its Lessons and Results. Interview with the General," p. 4.

32. William Booth, "Holiness. An Address at The Conference," p. 194.

33. William Booth, "God and You!" *The Christian Mission Magazine* (February 1875):34.

34. William Booth, "Letter from William Booth to the Brethren and Sisters Labouring for Jesus in Connection with the Dunedin Hall Christian Mission, Edinburgh," p. 103. It is important to note that Booth's concept of ministry within the Church, which he shared with Catherine Booth, included men and women engaged in that ministry. This position was clarified as early as The Christian Mission minutes of 1870 in Section XII of those minutes entitled "Female Preachers." (The Minutes of the First Conference of The Christian Mission, 1870.)

35. Sandall, *The History of The Salvation Army*, 1: 112.

36. William Booth, "Holiness. An Address at the Conference," p. 193.

37. Edward H. Sugden, ed., *Wesley's Standard Sermons*, 2 vols. (London: The Epworth Press, 1966), 2:446-448.

38. William Booth, "Letter from William Booth to the Brethren and Sisters Labouring for Jesus in Connection with the Dunedin Hall Christian Mission, Edinburgh," p. 105.

39. Ibid.

40. Ibid.

41. Minutes from the First Conference of The Christian Mission, 1870, pp. 16-17. The Conference of 1876 clarified the meaning of the doctrine of sanctification in this way: "Resolved that the following definitions of the doctrines numbered 9 and 10 in our list of *Doctrines* be printed and issued to all our members. That is to say—We believe that after conversion there remain in the heart of a believer inclinations to evil or roots of bitterness, which, unless overpowered by Divine Grace, produce actual sin, but that these evil tendencies can be entirely taken away by the Spirit of God, and the whole heart thus cleansed from everything contrary to the will of God, or entirely sanctified, will then produce the fruits of the Spirit only. And we believe that persons thus entirely sanctified may by the power of God be kept unblameable and unreprovable before Him. Moved by Railton. Seconded by Garner" (Minutes of the Conference of The Christian Mission, 1876.)

42. William Booth, "Holiness. An Address at the Conference," p. 194.

43. Ibid.

44. See William Booth, "The Imitation of Jesus Christ, No. I," p. 9. See also William Booth, "Holiness, An Address at the Conference," p. 197; William Booth, "Rise and Fall," p. 2; William Booth, *The General's Letters, 1885* (London: International Headquarters, 1890), p. 80; William Booth, "The Christ-Man," *Full Salvation* 9 (December 1892):377; William Booth, *Purity of Heart*, pp. 42-45, 88; Sandall, *The History of The Salvation Army*, 1 :9. In the latter reference Sandall wrote that "at Gateshead, too, William and Catherine Booth decided that it was incumbent upon them to set forth definitely and

regularly the doctrine of Full Salvation. With John Wesley they had come to the conclusion that the very object of the Atonement was the conquest and removal of indwelling evil, and that the heart could be purified from its evil tendencies which would otherwise prove too strong for it and render it the helpless prey of every passing temptation."

William Booth, like John Wesley, did not believe that sanctification was some kind of mystical total perfectionism. As soon as the doctrine was propagated, there were immediately misconceptions about the doctrine. Therefore, Booth found himself defining the doctrine not only positively in terms of what sanctification is, but also negatively in terms of what sanctification is not. This latter method of definition became necessary from the outset in order to assail misunderstandings and misgivings. "Now don't let us get into confusion by mistaking each other. We don't say *without imperfection with the possibility of falling* .... Nor is it merely *without deliberate sin*" (William Booth, "Holiness. An Address at the Conference," p. 195).

He constantly affirmed that the blessing of sanctification was intended for every believer. In *The East London Evangelist* he wrote that 'Justification through the blood of Christ is a blessing of untold value, but sanctification through the Spirit is of equal worth and of everlasting necessity. Without holiness no man shall see the Lord" (William Booth, "What Are You Going to Do in 1869?" p. 51). Because he was convinced that holiness was for every believer, and that the believer was missing a vital experience who did not enjoy sanctification, he often became rather uncompromising and demanding when preaching or writing on the subject. "Get it. ... You will never rightly understand it until you have it. Like all other problems in religious experience it must be felt to be understood. Get it" (William Booth, "Holiness. An Address at the Conference," p. 196).

45. In 1877 Booth wrote that "It seems to me that there is a large amount of uncertainty abroad amongst us on this subject. Many of our own people seem to live in what may be called an indefinite land: they are all uncertainty and fear. If you ask the question, Have you got the clean heart? Has the Lord made, and does He keep you holy? You can get no distinct answer either one way or the other" (William Booth, "Holiness. An Address at the Conference," p. 193).

46. Sandall, *The History of The Salvation Army*, 2: 128. See also Sandall, *The History of The Salvation Army*, 1 :209. There Sandall made reference to the fact that one of the most prominent holiness teachers and authors of the nineteenth century, Asa Mahan, spoke at Salvation Army holiness meetings. See also William Booth, "Go!" *All the World* 1 (November 1884), p. 4. There he wrote: "They already know something; their own consciences, illuminated by the Spirit of God, which enlightens all men, have taught them something .... And then tell them what they don't know—your proclamation of Full

Salvation through the Blood of the Lamb!" It is of historic interest to note that the tradition of teaching the doctrine of holiness regularly has been maintained in The Salvation Army.

47. Quoted in Sandall, *The History of The Salvation Army*, 1:209.
48. William Booth, "Letter from William Booth to the Brethren and Sisters Labouring for Jesus in Connection with the Dunedin Hall Christian Mission, Edinburgh," p. 104.
49. Ibid., pp. 104-105.
50. William Booth, "Holiness. An Address at the Conference," p. 198.

CHAPTER II

STAGE TWO: THE MINISTRY AND THEOLOGY OF
WILLIAM BOOTH TO 1889-1890

1. Quoted in Sandall, *The History of The Salvation Army*, 1:230.
2. William Booth, "Our New Name," p. l.
3. See Roland Robertson, "The Salvation Army: The Persistence of Sectarianism,"in Brian R. Wilson, ed. *Patterns of Sectarianism* (London: Heinemann Educational Books, 1967), p. 75. Robertson himself has raised this question, and he mentioned in his article that it has been suggested, but never proved, that Booth consciously established the Army on the model of papal authority in the Roman Catholic Church. See also Railton, *Heathen England*, p. 29.
4. William Booth, *The General's Letters*, 1885, p . 52. Note that Booth elaborated upon this theme in a chapter entitled "The Spirit of Holy Warfare" in his book entitled *The Seven Spirits; or, What I Teach My Officers* (London: The Salvation Army Book Department, 1907), pp. 52-69.
5. William Booth, "What is The Salvation Army?" *The War Cry* 33 (July 1912):2. When questioned why this authoritarian system was established to be the means by which to operate The Salvation Army, Booth responded with various answers. He usually explained that the first reason was a practical one: the earliest converts in the East London were the disorganized and hopeless mass of the poor. Among them were drunkards, prostitutes, and skeptics. Booth believed that these people needed the discipline of an autocratic system, both for their own sakes and for the effectual work of the Army. Second, Booth was encouraged by the fact that The Salvation Army was expanding its work rapidly after its inception. He held that the growing ministry of The Salvation Army needed a central authority for its efficient operations which were increasingly more numerous and complicated. A third reason given by Booth for the autocratic control of The Salvation Army was one of self-fulfilling prophecy—it worked. Booth stressed this

reason in 1890 in his *In Darkest England and the Way Out*. His interpretation was that the system had worked quite efficiently up to that point in Army history. He wrote: "But our Army system is a great indisputable fact, so much so that our enemies sometimes reproach us with it. That it should be possible to create an Army Organization, and to secure faithful execution daily is indeed a wonder. ... It is notorious that we can send an officer from London, possessed of no extraordinary ability, to take command of any corps in the world, with a certainty that he will find soldiers eager to do his bidding, and without a thought of disputing his commands, so long as he continues faithful to the orders and regulations under which his men are enlisted" (p. viii).

A fourth reason for the autocratic structure of The Salvation Army was that unity was essential to the warfare of redemption, and Booth maintained that the surest way to insure unity was through such a structure. He assumed that autocracy and unity and harmony go together. He was convinced that God raised him up to be the central leader and authority of The Salvation Army, and he was further convinced that it was the joy of Salvationists "to accept my direction. And more still, their own experience has given them confidence in my integrity, discrimination, and judgment" ("Fifty Years' Salvation Service: Some of Its Lessons and Results. Interview with The General," p. 2). That direction to which he referred was fundamentally direction as to the war of redemption which he was sure was being waged by him and his people. Unity was essential to that warfare. "But such combination or oneness of action will only be possible with oneness of direction. If all are to act together all must act on one plan, and therefore all must act under one head" (William Booth, "What Is The Salvation Army? *The War Cry*, p. 2). Booth often stressed this reason. It was critical to him. For example, in 1885 he wrote: "The time is not far distant when these three great forces, superstition, infidelity, and godliness, will be face to face in the great final conflict for the possession of the earth and all the people that are on the face of it. Then will the value of unity be realized. When that terrible day shall come think of the courage and the strength, and the faith that will be derived from the united action of such a million Salvationists as we have hinted at above" (William Booth, *The General's Letters, 1885*, p. 54).

Reflecting his disdain for some disorderly approach to the necessary task of redemption, Booth wrote: "And then, my comrades, how advantageous union is for attacking the world. The conquest of the nations is a herculean business. The reason so little headway has been made hitherto has been largely owing to the fragmentary manner in which the attempt has been made. Every man and every penny will be required. We are weak, and are likely to be so for some time; but united, even today, The Army is not an insignificant force. Let us be faithful, and we shall be strong and go forward to victory" (Ibid., p.

55). Elaborating upon this theme, he wrote: "But we are not for destruction. We are for restoration—the restoration of man to God. To accomplish this a force is required—a stupendous force—the more stupendous the better. It must be a force bound with the closest earthly and strongest heavenly bonds; one doctrine, one spirit, one government, one end all prostrated in obedience to the Divine Head—the God and Father of us all. This means submission. This means obedience. We have spoken of difficulties. What are the real difficulties that lie in the way of the realization of this one Army covering the earth and doing its share at least in the conquest of it for its rightful King?" (Ibid., p. 63).

Finally, that structure was also an eschatological sign—it was a present sign of the unity that will be manifested in the kingdom of God and in the millennium. It was, for Booth, a present physical sign of an ultimate spiritual reality. "Union is evidently God's plan, seeking it is to prevail in Heaven. There will be one Army in the New Jerusalem. They won't say there, 'I am of Paul,' or 'I am of Apollos,' but all will be of one heart and of one soul. The New Jerusalem model is for us down here. Let us get as near to its realization as we can" (Ibid., p. 52). Booth constantly claimed that "the feeling that God intends us to continue forever one Army, one family, one Kingdom, has become an enthusiastic conviction in the hearts of Officers and Soldiers, and I believe there are multitudes under our colours who are willing to suffer and die to maintain it" (Ibid., p. 53).

6. So important was this principle to Booth that he lost from The Salvation Army members of his immediate family who in one way or another disagreed with that principle. But Booth maintained that the universal autocratic structure of The Salvation Army was a higher principle than the keeping of unity or allegiance within his own family. The family secessions from The Salvation Army caused the greatest distress for Booth, second only to the death of Catherine Booth in 1890, and death of his daughter, Emma, in 1903. Among these secessions were Ballington Booth, a son of William and Catherine Booth, and his wife who resigned from The Salvation Army on January 31, 1896; Catherine Booth, a daughter of William and Catherine Booth, and her husband who resigned from The Salvation Army on January 10, 1902; and Herbert Booth, a son of William and Catherine Booth, and his wife who resigned from The Salvation Army on February 2, 1902. For further information about this see chapter 11 entitled "Three Who Left" in Green, *The Life and Ministry of William Booth: Founder of The Salvation Army.*

7. William Booth, *In Darkest England and The Way Out*, p. 242.

8. Ibid.

9. Ibid.

10. William Booth, "The General's Address at the Wesleyan Conference," *The War Cry* 1 (August 1880):1.

11. Needham, "Redemption and Social Reformation: A Theological Study of William Booth and His Movement," p. 126. See the Rev. Benjamin Field, *The Student's Handbook of Christian Theology*, ed., John C. Symans, with an Introduction by L. Tyerman (New York: The Methodist Book Concern, 1886).

12. For some discussion of the differences between *Booth's Doctrines and Disciplines* and Field's *Handbook* see Needham, "Redemption and Social Reformation: A Theological Study of William Booth and His Movement," pp. 125-129, 141. Soon after the publication of *Doctrines and Disciplines*, Booth was severely criticized with the allegation that he was attempting to teach secretly to officers a system that he dare not openly avow. Booth immediately ordered a published edition of the doctrines and their explanations to be made available to the public exactly as they had first appeared for private instruction, with an additional section setting forth more clearly his position on the doctrine of holiness. "Accompanying this edition was an emphatic protest that the only reason the book had not been publicly circulated was that The Salvation Army had desired most earnestly to avoid any appearance of condemning or opposing the teachings of others" (Sandall, *The History of The Salvation Army*, 2: 129).

13. Wiggins, The History of The Salvation Army, 4:240. The culmination of royal acceptance, however, came on June 24, 1904 when Booth was received at Buckingham Palace by King Edward VII.

14. The finest account of the beginning of the work of The Salvation Army in America and of the growth of The Salvation Army in America is Edward H. McKinley, *Marching to Glory: The History of The Salvation Army in the United States of America, 1880-1980* (San Francisco: Harper & Row, Publishers, 1980). Regarding the growth of The Salvation Army in America, on p. 37 Professor McKinley writes: "In the summer of 1880 there were eight corps in the United States, six of them in Philadelphia: in the summer of 1890 there were 410 corps in thirty-five states." A second and expanded edition of this book was published by William B. Eerdmans Publishing Company in 1995 with the revised title *Marching to Glory: The History of The Salvation Army in the United States, 1880-1992.*

15. Robertson, "The Salvation Army: The Persistence of Sectarianism," p.91.

16. Charles Booth, *Life and Labour of the People in London*, 17 vols. (London: MacMillan Company, Ltd., 1902) 1:124-125.

17. Ibid., p. 126. The year 1886 was the year of greatest growth in The Salvation Army in England and abroad. Arch Wiggins, admittedly not an objective observer of Salvation Army history, does provide some light on the subject when he reported the following growth for that year: "An increase of 476 brought the world total of corps to 2,262 and an increase of 1,492 brought the world total of officers to 5,684. The Army itself was a third larger than it was at the beginning of the year, and its forward steps were much more striking

and important than those of any previous year in its history. During 1886 no fewer than148,000 persons confessed conversion at the penitent-form in the United Kingdom alone. The Bishop of London, in summing up the results of the Church of England's efforts in the metropolis, had mentioned, among other facts, that it had assembled in its London churches11,000 persons on weeknights; thereupon the Army made a survey to discover that on one ordinary weeknight in November 16,746 persons had gathered in its London barracks, with no other attraction than the Gospel of Christ" (Wiggins, *The History of The Salvation Army*, 4: 184-185. See also Coutts, *No Discharge in this War*, pp. 36, 42).

By 1890 with the inauguration of the Darkest England Scheme, William Booth relied upon the growth of The Salvation Army as an obvious and positive witness to the potential success of his program. He believed that such statistics substantiated both the truth of the theology that he proclaimed and the claims of success that the Army was making toward the salvation of the world. In *In Darkest England and the Way Out* he reported that there were around the world a total of 2,874 corps, 896 outposts, 9,416 officers, and a total annual circulation of Salvation Army literature of 37,400,000 (pp. iii-iv).

Three years later, in 1893, a Northern European Congress was held to celebrate the work of The Salvation Army in France, Switzerland, Belgium, Holland, Germany, Denmark, Sweden, Norway, and Finland. From 1890 to 1893, "the number of corps had been increased from 287 to 896; officers from 500 to 1,800; social institutions from 1 rescue home to 3, and 19 other centers, including food depots, shelters, factories and labour yards had been established" (Wiggins, *The History of The Salvation Army*, 4: 153).

18. William Booth, *The General's Letters, 1885*, p. 58. Booth appealed to that growth when, during the summer of 1886, he said, "You can judge whether a movement that was not of God could have made the progress that this has done in the last four years" (William Booth, "The General's Address at Exeter Hall on Monday Evening," p. 9). He also stated his oft-recited theological position regarding the development of The Salvation Army when he said this: "As to the results of all this work, you see some of it before you. The Army is its own result. It is a self-made affair: it has evolved out of itself. It is the natural rule of multiplication and increase—human and divine, for I contend that God has taken men into partnership into everything that He does in this world, or nearly everything .... just so with the saving of souls. Let man do his part and God will do His part" (Ibid.).

19. William Booth, *Religion for Every Day*, p. 43.

20. Ibid., p. 133. See also William Booth, *In Darkest England and the Way Out*, p. 92; William Booth, 'The General To Backsliders from the Ranks of The Salvation Army, and to Backsliders Everywhere," *The War Cry* 13 January 1892):9-10; William Booth, "Christianity on Fire, No. V," p. 9; "Fifty Years'

Salvation Service: Some of Its Lessons and Results. Interview with The General," p. 8; William Booth, "All Things New," *All the World* 11 January 1895):5; William Booth, *Religion for Every Day*, p.20.

21. William Booth, *The General's Letters, 1885*. p. 102.
22. William Booth, "Salvation for Both Worlds," p. 1.
23. William Booth, "The Imitation of Jesus Christ, No. IV," *The War Cry*, 14 (October 1893):9. See also William Booth, *The General's Letters, 1885*, p. 154; William Booth, "Salvation for Both Worlds," p. 2; "Fifty Years' Salvation Service: Some of Its Lessons and Results. Interview with The General," pp. 4-5; William Booth, *To My Officers: A Letter from the General on His Eightieth Birthday* (St. Albans: The Salvation Army Printing Works, 1909), pp. 12-13.
24. William Booth, "Christianity on Fire, No. I." *The War Cry* 13 (April 1892):9.
25. Chadwick, *The Victorian Church*, 1 :6.
26. William Booth, *The General's Letters, 1885*, p. 156.
27. "Fifty Years' Salvation Service: Some of Its Lessons and Results. Interview with The General," p. 3.
28. William Booth, *The General's Letters, 1885*, p. 74.
29. William Booth, "The Christ-Man," pp. 377-380.
30. William Booth, *The General's Letters, 1885*, p. 107.
31. Ibid., p. 74.
32. William Booth, "The Imitation of Jesus Christ, No. I," p. 9.
33. William Booth, "Salvation for Both Worlds," p. 1.
34. William Booth, "The Crown of Thorns," p. 433.
35. Ibid. See also William Booth, "The Imitation of Jesus Christ, No. I," p.9.
36. William Booth, "The Christ-Man," p. 379.
37. William Booth, "The Imitation of Jesus Christ, No. II," p. 8. See also William Booth, *The General's Letters, 1885*, p. 13.
38. William Booth, "The Imitation of Jesus Christ, No. III," *The War Cry*, 14 (October 1893):1.
39. William Booth, "Go!," p. 3.
40. William Booth, "The Imitation of Jesus Christ, No. III," p. 2. See also William Booth, "The Christ-Man," p. 379; William Booth, "Christianity on Fire, No. I," p. 9; William Booth, "The Crown of Thorns," p. 434; William Booth, "The Imitation of Jesus Christ, No. I," p. 9; William Booth, "The Imitation of Jesus Christ, No. II," p. 9.
41. St. John Ervine, *God's Soldier: General William Booth*, 1:478. G. Kitson Clark wrote that the streets of England "could still be the scenes of brutal and unchecked violence, as The Salvation Army found when it started operations in the 'eighties' " (G. Kitson Clark, *The Making of Victorian England* [Cambridge, Massachusetts: Harvard University Press, 1962], p. 140).
42. William Booth, *The General's Letters, 1885*, p. 117.
43. William Booth, "Christianity on Fire, No. VII." p. 9.

44. William Booth, "What is The Salvation Army," *The War Cry*, p. 2.
45. William Booth, "Salvation for Both Worlds," p. 2.
46. Ibid.
47. William Booth, "Besetting Sins," *The War Cry* 12 (March 1891):9.
48. William Booth, "Fight!" *All the World* 1 (May 1885): 112.
49. William Booth, "Salvation for Both Worlds," p. 2.
50. William Booth, *The General's Letters, 1885*, p. 35. See also William Booth, "The Imitation of Jesus Christ, No. I," p. 9. Booth's doctrine of ministry within the Church still included women and men participating equally in that ministry. This remained an important issue for William Booth, and especially for Catherine Booth. For example, see the following: William Booth, "On Salvation Women," *The Field Officer* 9 (September 1901):422-424; William Booth, "Letters from the General to the Soldiers of The Salvation Army. More About Women's Rights," *The Field Officer* 9 (November 1901):513-514; and Mildred Duff, "Our First General and the Place He Gave to Women," *The Field Officer* 20 (October 1912):373-376. See Andrew Mark Eason's extensive work on this subject in his book entitled *Women in God's Army: Gender and Equality in the Early Salvation Army* (Waterloo, Ontario, Canada: Wilfrid Laurier University Press, 2003).
51. William Booth, "Christianity on Fire, No. I," p. 9. This imagery became important to Booth in his later theology. In this same article William Booth wrote the following: "My heart is full of new plans as well as desires, but the main business at the onset is to get 100,000 soldiers to join hands and heart together to beseech the Throne of God for a Pentecostal outpouring of Fire, as real and as practical and as glorious in its results as that which came on Peter and the rest of the Apostles in Jerusalem two thousand years ago."

   In another article he wrote the following: "Oh, you officers, you soldiers, my children, may I not call you?—the hope of the Army, nay, I think I may say (for all men know I think so) the hope of Christendom— the hope of the world! You see where your work is, and you see where your strength lies. Seek that strength if you have it not; cherish it where it is possessed; spread it amongst your comrades, amongst the crowds who love us, though not entered on our rolls. Above all, go out with it blazing in your hearts. And, in its power, repeat, with mightier emphasis, the triumphs of the Apostolic Age in gathering to Christ thousands, tens of thousands, hundreds of thousands of souls" (William Booth, "Christianity on Fire, No. VII," p. 9).

   In another article of similar language William Booth wrote: "Think of the running to and fro, the rumors, the gossip, the sensational stories produced by that Pentecostal Fire which set Jerusalem in that hallelujah blaze! Everybody wanted to hear about it, to understand how it originated . . .. But a corps on Fire will present the most convincing argument for the supernatural world, will do more to make men believe in God and Calvary, heaven and hell and judgment than all the arguments that can be conceived, or the books that can be written, and prove the biggest and most effective advertisement for the claims of God that can be brought before the attention of men. If you want to get sinners into your barracks, get the Fire. Oh, I have proved it again and again! Red-hot meetings will bring you congregations, will form a greater "draw" than all the posters and catch bills and other attractions put together. The people will come—cannot help but come, nothing will keep them away. They may scoff at your doctrines, be disgusted with the noise, disapprove the excitement, and be cut to the heart with the truth, but they will come nevertheless" (William Booth, "Christianity on Fire, No. IV," *The War Cry* 13 [May 1892]:10).

Later in this study it will be noted that the establishment of the Kingdom of God became essential to the later theology of William Booth. The analogy of The Salvation Army and the Church in the New Testament was useful to him in that part of his theology. He once wrote that the struggle to establish the kingdom of God on earth which would result in the millennium "will be carried on with greater vigor, although, in substance, on the same lines as those on which the Apostles fought and died." (William Booth, "The Millennium; or, The Ultimate Triumph of Salvation Army Principles," *All the World* 6 [August 1890]:337).

52. William Booth, "Salvation for Both Worlds," p. 6.

53. William Booth, "The General's Address at Exeter Hall on Monday Evening," p. 9.

54. Sandall, *The History of The Salvation Army*, 2: 125. For further information regarding the distinction of the sect from the Church see Ernst Troeltsch, *The Social Teaching of the Christian Churches*, 2 vols. (New York: Harper and Row, Publishers, 1960) 1:421-435; Max Weber, *The Protestant Ethic and the Spirit of Capitalism* (New York: Charles Scribner's Sons, 1958); Max Weber, "The Protestant Sects and the Spirit of Capitalism," in Hans H. Gerth and C. Wright Mills, eds., *From Max Weber: Essays in Sociology* (New York: Oxford University Press, 1974), pp. 302-322. However, for an excellent analysis of The Salvation Army as a sectarian movement see Roland Robertson, "The Salvation Army: the Persistence of Sectarianism," in Brian R. Wilson, ed. *Patterns of Sectarianism* (London: Heinemann Educational Books, 1967), pp. 49-105.

It should also be noted that Bramwell Booth, the eldest son of William and Catherine Booth and the second General of The Salvation Army, articulated that same sentiment of his father's regarding sectarianism when he stated that "The Salvation Army has set aside those observances and differences of government which have divided the church into sects. In spirit and in truth it is part of the universal Church of Christ, and is none the less in authority

and in standing a church—that is, part of the body of Christ upon earth"
(Quoted in Sandall, *The History of The Salvation Army*, 2: 125).

55. William Booth, "What is The Salvation Army?" *The Contemporary Review*,
p. 181. Cardinal Manning was critical of Booth at this point, and he believed
that The Salvation Army would become a sect. In his article entitled "The
Salvation Army," Manning stated: "Nevertheless, we have a conviction that
The Salvation Army will either become a sect, or it will melt away. This
world is not the abode of disembodied spirits. The history of Christianity
abundantly proves that neither the human intellect nor the human will can
alone perpetuate any teaching without change. Nor can human authority or
human obedience perpetuate itself without an organization which compacts
and sustains both" (Henry Edward Manning, "The Salvation Army," *The
Contemporary Review* 41 [August 1882]:341).

56. William Booth, "What Is The Salvation Army?" *The Contemporary Review*,
p. 182. For other references to William Booth's thinking on this matter
see the following: William Booth, "The General's Address at the Wesleyan
Conference," p. 1; William Booth, "The Majors' Council. Notes of the
General's Address," *The War Cry* 3 (November 1882):3; William Booth, "The
General's New Year Address to Officers," *The War Cry* (17 January 1883): 1-4.

57. Robertson, "The Salvation Army: The Persistence of Sectarianism," p.66. The
most extensive work on The Salvation Army and the sacraments is R. David
Rightmire, *Sacraments and The Salvation Army: Pneumatological Foundations*
(Metuchen, NJ: The Scarecrow Press, Inc., 1990). See also Andrew Mark Eason,
"The Salvation Army and the Sacraments in Victorian Britain: Retracing the
Steps to Non-Observance" *Fides et Historia* 41 (Summer/Fall 2009): 51-71.

58. William Booth, *Religion for Every Day*, p. 130.

59. Quoted in Sandall, *The History of The Salvation Army*, 2: 130.

60. Begbie, *The Life of General William Booth* 1 :377.

61. William Booth, *Religion for Every Day*, p. 102.

62. Ibid., pp. 164-165. One of William Booth's most interesting statements on
the sacraments can be found in his article entitled "The General's New Year
Address to Officers," *The War Cry* (17 January 1883): 1-4.

63. The two most concise works by William Booth on the doctrine of sanctification by faith are these: *Purity of Heart*, and *A Ladder to Holiness*. Beyond
these works, he wrote numerous articles on the doctrine, and preached the
doctrine often.

64. William Booth, "Christianity on Fire, No. IV," *The War Cry* 13 (May 1892):9-
10. See also William Booth, *The General's Letters, 1885*, p. 35. Booth wrote
the following on *Orders and Regulations for Field Officers*: "The F.O. must
have been converted or changed by the power of the Holy Spirit from the
old, worldly, selfish, sinful nature: and not only must he thus have received a
new heart, but he must have the Holy Spirit living in that heart, possessing it,

and working through it, to will and to do the good pleasure of God" (Quoted in Begbie, *The Life of General William Booth* 2: 147-148).

65. William Booth, *To My Officers: A Letter from The General on His Eightieth Birthday*, p. 33.
66. William Booth, *Purity of Heart*, pp. 71-72.
67. There are many examples of this, but the following will suffice: See Catherine Booth, "Do Something," *The Salvation News* July 1880):1; Catherine Booth, "The Holy Ghost," *All The World* 16 June 1900): 341; an article by one of the Booths' sons-in-law, Arthur Booth-Clibborn, "The Pentecostal Programme," *All The World* 11 June 1895):402; See also "The Conquest of the World," *All the World* 17 (February 1901):60; and "As It Was in the Beginning!" *All The World* 17 July 1901) 340, 342.
68. Ernest R. Sandeen, *The Roots of Fundamentalism* (Chicago: The University of Chicago Press, 1970).
69. Ibid., p. 39.
70. James Black, *New Forms of Old Faith* (London, 1948), p. 232, quoted in George Shepperson, "The Comparative Study of Millenarian Movements," *Millennial Dreams in Action*, Sylvia R. Thrupp, ed. (The Hague: Mouton, 1962), p. 44.
71. Donald W. Dayton, *Discovering an Evangelical Heritage* (New York: Harper & Row, Publishers, 1976), p. 125.
72. Ibid., p. 126.
73. William Booth, *The General's Letters, 1885*, p. 99. See also p. 37; William Booth, "Hints to Soul Winners," p. 125; William Booth, "Go!" p. 1; William Booth, "Memorable Challenge!" p. 9; and "Fifty Years' Salvation Service: Some of Its Lessons and Results. Interview with The General," p. 7.
74. See William Booth, *The General's Letters, 1885*, p. 60.
75. See especially the following: William Booth, "Our New Name," p. 3; William Booth, *The General's Letters, 1885*, pp. 18,33, 172, 195; William Booth, "Forward," *The War Cry* 8 (January 1887):9; William Booth, "The General's Address," *The War Cry* 8 (January 1887):9; William Booth, "How We Began," an introduction to George Railton, *Twenty One Years Salvation Army* (London: the Salvation Army Publishing Offices, 1887), p. 23; William Booth, *In Darkest England and the Way Out*, p. 284; William Booth, "Christianity on Fire, No. III," *The War Cry* 13 (May 1892):9; William Booth, *To My Officers: A Letter from The General on His Eightieth Birthday*, p. 19; William Booth, "The Army Mother," *The War Cry* 31 (October 1910):9; William Booth, "Memorable Challenge!" p. 9; William Booth, "What is The Salvation Army?" *The War Cry*, p. 2; William Booth, *International Social Council Addresses*, 1911 (London: The Salvation Army Printing Works, 1912), p. 52; William Booth, *Religion for Every Day*, 14, 27, 52-53.

See both biographical and historical evaluation of Booth's devotion to The Salvation Army in these sources: Begbie, *The Life of General William*

Booth, 1 :415; 2:4, 172; Sandall, *The History of The Salvation Army*, 2:2; Wiggins, *The History of The Salvation Army*, 4: 174; 5: 146.

This statement, written by Booth in *The General's Letters, 1885*, p. 73, to Salvationists gives one a typical picture of Booth's single mindedness regarding The Salvation Army, and the work that he believed The Salvation Army was destined to carry out. Booth said: "Hold on, comrades! Nay, take fresh hold. Let us review the reasons for our conflict. We fight not for one man, not for one garrison. We fight for the deliverance of a whole world. The destiny of millions, nay, I verily believe of hundreds of millions, is hanging in the balance—depending to an awful extent on the enthusiastic, skillful, and self-sacrificing, conduct, and maintenance of this war."

William Booth constantly impressed upon his hearers and readers that every person's vocation was of "divine appointment," (William Booth, *Religion for Every Day*, p. 14), and for that reason, one's vocation must be pursued carefully and diligently. Chadwick notes in *The Victorian Church* (2: 146) that "The most marked character in Victorian religion is the sense of vocation, and this sense carried with it a powerful sense of the sacredness of time and the sin of wasting it." Booth certainly possessed this Victorian sense of vocation, and constantly encouraged his readers and hearers to understand their vocations.

76. William Booth, *The General's Letters, 1885*, p. 22.
77. Ibid., pp. 142-145. Booth "believed that it was possible to bring men and women of every degree and temperament into the fold of The Salvation Army, and he even dared, in certain moments of enthusiasm, to think that he himself might live to accomplish this consummation" (Begbie, *The Life of General William Booth* 2:252). See also pp. 251, 359, 402, 403; McKinley, *Marching to Glory*, p. 33. Shortly before his death in 1912, Booth said, "I am more confident than ever that Salvation is the only hope for the world. Were it not for Salvation and the Salvation of The Salvation Army, I should think that the probability was that the world was on its way to universal suicide" (Begbie, *The Life of General William Booth* 2:417).
78. William Booth, "What Is The Salvation Army?" *The War Cry*, p. 2.
79. William Booth, *To My Officers: A Letter From the General on His Eightieth Birthday*, pp. 14-15. See also pp. 16-17, 54.
80. William Booth, "The Imitation of Jesus Christ, No. III," p. 1
81. William Booth, *In Darkest England and The Way Out*, pp. 44-45. See also William Booth, "Salvation for Both Worlds," p. 3.
82. William Booth, *In Darkest England and The Way Out*, p. 79.
83. Ibid., p. 80.
84. For a long statement of this, which was typical of Booth, see William Booth, *To My Officers: A Letter from The General on His Eightieth Birthday*, pp. 23-26.

85. Referring to theological debates which were common during his day, and especially to millennial debates, Booth said, "About these things, however, we have neither time nor disposition to argue" (William Booth, "The Millennium; or, The Ultimate Triumph of Salvation Army Principles," p. 342).

86. William Booth, *In Darkest England and The Way Out*, p. 80. This was the same phrase that he used to signify the millennium in "The Millennium; or, The Ultimate Triumph of Salvation Army Principles."

87. Ibid., p. 342. The front cover of *The War Cry*, 32 (March 18, 1911) showed Salvationists going on a road, and the signpost of the road read: "Straight on to the New Heaven and the New Earth."

88. William Booth, "The Millennium: or, The Ultimate Triumph of Salvation Army Principles," p. 338.

89. Ibid.

90. William Booth, "Forward," p. 9.

91. William Booth, *The General's Letters, 1885*, pp. 32-33.

92. William Booth, "All Things New," p. 4.

93. William Booth, "The Millennium; or, The Ultimate Triumph of Salvation Army Principles," p. 338.

94. Ibid.

95. Ibid.

96. William Booth, *The General's Letters, 1885*, p. 61. The importance of love as a vehicle for the ministry of The Salvation Army and for the ultimate victory of establishing the Kingdom of God on earth is readily seen in the *Orders and Regulations for Field Officers*, which were written by William Booth. In that work Booth affirmed that "this invincible method of securing victory is possible to every Officer alike. All cannot equally solo, or speak eloquently, or invent new plans, but all can love. Love is a gift that grows with its exercise. The more an Officer loves, the more ability he has to love. Let every Officer prove the truth of this sentiment by putting it to practice" (Quoted in Begbie, *The Life of General William Booth* 2: 152).

97. William Booth, "The Millennium; or, The Ultimate Triumph of Salvation Army Principles," p. 338.

98. Ibid., p. 339.

99. William Booth, "A Passion for Souls," The Conqueror 1 (October 1892), p. 275. See also William Booth, "The Christ-Man," p. 278: "Oh, the consolation of love! For Him to commune with you—talk with you—fight the devil for you. He will take care of you."

100. William Booth, *Religion for Every Day*, pp. 60-61. See also William Booth, *In Darkest England and the Way Out*, p. 217. It is interesting to note that this goal is still engendered in the officers and soldiers of The Salvation Army today. The "Articles of War" contain the doctrinal and personal commitment to which Salvationists must adhere. The "Articles of War"

read, in part, "I do here declare that I will never treat any woman, child, or other person, whose life, comfort, or happiness may be placed within my power, in any oppressive, cruel, or cowardly manner, but that I will protect such from evil and danger so far as I can, and promote to the uttermost of my ability, their present welfare and eternal Salvation." See *Salvation Army Ceremonies* (London: Salvationist Publishing and Supplies, 1966), pp. 2-5.

101. William Booth, "The Millennium; or, The Ultimate Triumph of Salvation Army Principles," p. 339.

102. Ibid.

103. Ibid., p. 342. Booth believed that one of the greatest errors among people was that love could be self-motivated, could be acquired, manufactured, or fashioned apart from God. He believed that people inherently sensed the need for love, but they did not realize the source of that love, and, when manufactured, much love soon turned into self-interest. Such love required for redeeming the world "can only come from that God, whose nature is love, and through the Christ Who gave Himself to death, in order that from His Cross there might flow out to all men the Water of Life" (Ibid.).

104. William Booth, "All Things New," pp. 4-6.

105. William Booth, "The Millennium; or, The Ultimate Triumph of Salvation Army Principles," p. 339. See also William Booth, *The General's Letters, 1885*, p. 123.

106. William Booth, "All Things New," p. 3.

107. William Booth, "The Millennium; or, The Ultimate Triumph of Salvation Army Principles," p. 340. On one occasion William Booth expressed to a women that he thought all five of her sons should be Salvation Army officers. The woman asked Booth what would become of business in this world if everyone became officers in The Salvation Army, to which Booth responded, " 'The business of this world, you mean, I presume. Oh, let the business of this world take care of itself,' I replied. 'My business is to get the world saved; if this involves the standing still of the looms and the shutting up of the factories, and the staying of the sailing of ships, let them all stand still. When we have got everybody converted they can go on again, and we shall be able to keep things going then by working half time and have the rest to spend in loving one another and worshipping God' " (William Booth, *The General's Letters, 1885*, p. 21).

108. William Booth, "The Millennium; or, The Ultimate Triumph of Salvation Army Principles," pp. 340-341. Booth is unclear here as to the degree of perfectability of this earth during the millennium. He appears to hold to the idea that there are some imperfections even during the millennium.

109. Eventually William Booth and The Salvation Army received recognition in England. These were three important events in the later years of Booth's life

which give evidence of such acceptance: in 1904 King Edward VII received William Booth in Buckingham Palace; in 1905 William Booth was granted both the Freedom of the City of London and the Freedom of the City of Nottingham; and in 1907 William Booth was given the D.C.L. degree from Oxford University.

110. William Booth, "An Interview with His Late Majesty King Edward VII," p.9.

111. William Booth, "Rise and Fall," p. 3.

112. Ibid.

113. William Booth, "Christianity on Fire, No. I," p. 9.

114. William Booth, "The Millennium; or, The Ultimate Triumph of Salvation Army Principles," p. 341.

115. Ibid.

116. Ibid.

117. Ibid., p. 342. For Booth's concept of physical illness and its treatment see William Booth, *The Doctrines and Disciplines of The Salvation Army* (London: International Headquarters, 1881), p. 24. See also Catherine Booth, "Hints in Health by the Water Treatment," in William Booth, *Orders and Regulations for Field Officers of The Salvation Army* (London: Salvation Army, 1888), pp. 617-624.

118. William Booth, "The Millennium; or, The Ultimate Triumph of Salvation Army Principles," p. 342.

119. William Booth, "Will You Let Me In?" *The War Cry* 33 (May 1912):2.

120. William Booth, "The Millennium; or, The Ultimate Triumph of Salvation Army Principles," p. 337.

121. William Booth, *The General's Letters, 1885*, p. 145.

122. The evidence is overwhelming that those who shared the hierarchical power with William Booth also shared much of his theology, and especially his theology regarding the kingdom of God. There are innumerable examples of this, but the following will suffice: For Catherine Booth see the following: Catherine Booth, "The Holy Ghost," *All The World* 16 (June 1900), pp. 339-342; Catherine Booth, "The Kingdom of Christ," *All The World* 1 (August 1885), pp. 183-184; and Catherine Booth, *Popular Christianity* (London: Salvation Army Book Depot, 1887), p. 197. For Bramwell Booth, a son and successor to William Booth as the next General of The Salvation Army, see Bramwell Booth, "Salvation Army," *Encyclopedia of Religion and Ethics*, 12 vols., James Hastings, ed. (New York: Charles Scribner's Sons, 1921), 11:151. For Evangeline Booth, a daughter and the fourth General of The Salvation Army, see Evangeline Booth, *Toward a Better World* (Garden City, New York: Doubleday, Doran and Company, 1928), p. 241. Evangeline Booth later wrote a song entitled "The World for God." For Arthur Booth-Clibborn, one of the Booths' sons-in-law (all the Booths' sons-in-law took the Booth name), see Arthur Booth-Clibborn, "The

Pentecostal Programme", *All The World* 11 June 1895), pp. 401-405. For John Lawley, one of Booth's early advisors and eventually a commissioner in The Salvation Army, see John Lawley, "Down With The Gates!" *The War Cry* 14 (October 1893), p. 12. John Lawley, "Down With The Gates!" *The War Cry* 14 (November 1893). p. 12. For Elijah Cadman, another advisor and commissioner in The Salvation Army, see Elijah Cadman, "The New Kingdom," *All The World* 11 July 1895). pp. 3-4.

Roland Robertson is correct in saying that during the history of The Salvation Army in Booth's lifetime, millennial teachings were important, and "from time to time the question of the millennium was viewed with some degree of urgency" (Roland Robertson, "The Salvation Army: The Persistence of Sectarianism," p. 71.)

However, nowhere is Booth's doctrine of redemption, his doctrine of the kingdom of God, and his postmillennial sympathies better expressed in practical ways than in the songs that were written by Salvationists. Many songs that were composed and sung by Salvationists around the world during Booth's lifetime expressed his theology of redemption that issued in the Kingdom of God and in the millennium. When Booth compiled various songs, he incorporated songs relating to redemption, the kingdom of God, or the millennium into a section of the songbook appropriately called "War Songs." See William Booth, comp., *The Salvation Army Songs.*

William Booth himself wrote four songs that were published, and all of them deal primarily with the theme of holiness. Many of the members of the Booth family wrote songs for The Salvation Army, and many people who were important to Booth, such as George Scott Railton, John Lawley, and Richard Slater, also wrote songs for The Salvation Army. See various songs and their backgrounds in Avery, *Companion to the Song Book of The Salvation Army*. See also William Booth, comp., *The Salvation Soldiers' Song Book* (Toronto: Salvation Army Publishing House, n.d.); song entitled "For The Lord We Go To War," *The Conqueror* 4 June 1895), pp. 247; Howard Chesham and Sallie Chesham, *Combat Songs Of The Salvation Army* (New York: Salvationist Publishing and Supplies, 1976).

Such songs, which were numerous, were not designed to give definitive limits to the theology that they contained. They were written to give practical expression to the vitality of the theology of William Booth and to the theology of The Salvation Army. In doing so, it became clear that Booth's speculations about the kingdom of God and the millennium were not theological abstractions that were remote from the hue and cry of Salvation Army officers and soldiers around the world. These songs were not theological treatises concerned with fine nuances of theology. They were songs for the faithful—they served the function of stimulating men and women to faith in God, and of encouraging men and women to engage in, and continue in, the holy war to which God had called them. For examples of these songs, see William Booth, comp., *The Salvation Army Songs*, song no. 559, verse 4 and chorus; song no. 577, verse 4; song no. 578, verse 5 and chorus; song no. 580, verse 3 and chorus.

CHAPTER III:

STAGE THREE: THE MINISTRY AND THEOLOGY OF WILLIAM BOOTH FROM 1889-1890

1. St. John Ervine, *God's Soldier: General William Booth*, 1:38.
2. Sandall, *The History of The Salvation Army*, 1:266. See Appendix "H" in Sandall, p. 265-266 for the entire program.
3. Sandall, *The History of The Salvation Army*, 1:196.
4. William Booth, "Our New Name," p. 1.
5. William Booth, "The General's Address at the Wesleyan Conference," p. 1.
6. H. J. Dyos and Michael Wolff, eds. *The Victorian City*, 2 vols. (London: Routledge and Kegan Paul, 1973) 2:595.
7. Coutts, *Bread for My Neighbour*, p. 107.
8. William Booth, "The General's Address," p. 9.
9. Clark, *The Making of Victorian England*, p. 32.
10. W. T. Stead, *The Star*, January 2, 1891, quoted in Sandall, 3:325.
11. Ibid. The following was noted in *The Victorian City* regarding the support that the London dock strike received from Salvationists and others: "Support from institution representatives such as Canon Barnett, Stewart Headlam, William Booth, and Cardinal Manning served both to give a sense of direction to public feeling, and to consolidate the positions of the institutions in the East End" (Dyos and Wolff, eds., *The Victorian City*, 2:595).
12. Booth refers to such people and groups often throughout *In Darkest England and the Way Out*.
13. Ibid., p. 2. Booth believed that he was now ready to improve on work being done.
14. Ibid., p. 16.
15. Ibid., p. 243.
16. See Bernard Watson, *Soldier Saint* (London: Hodder and Stoughton, 1970), chap. 17. This is the best biography available on George Scott Railton, and the seventeenth chapter records in detail Railton's opposition to The Salvation Army Assurance Society.
17. William Booth, "Will You Let Me In?" p. 2.
18. William Booth, "Salvation for Both Worlds," p. 3.
19. William Booth, *The General's Letters, 1885*, p. 150.
20. William Booth, *In Darkest England and the Way Out*, p. 36.

21. Catherine Booth, *Life and Death* (London: International Headquarters, 1890), p. 203.

22. "Fifty Years' Salvation Service: Some of Its Lessons and Results. Interview With The General," p. 5. See also Begbie, *The Life of General William Booth*, 1 :367. Begbie quoted from a letter from William Booth to Bramwell Booth written on August 27, 1876: "To go to college—the difficulty would arise, where? I know not. All except the Methodist Institutions are Calvinistic-cold-blooded-and while improving the mind, do, I fear, injure the heart." See also William Booth, *The General's Letters, 1885*, p.147.

23. William Booth, *In Darkest England and The Way Out*, p 36.

24. Ibid.

25. William Booth, "Salvation for Both Worlds," p. 2.

26. Ibid.

27. Coutts, *No Discharge in this War*, p. 102.

28. William Booth, "Salvation for Both Worlds," pp. 2-3.

29. Ibid., p. 2.

30. Ibid.

31. Ibid.

32. Ibid.

33. Needham, "Redemption and Social Reformation: A Theological Study of William Booth and His Movement," p. 80. Cardinal Manning, supporting Booth's plan, commended Booth both for his analysis of the social plight of London in the last quarter of the nineteenth century, and for his encompassing social program that addressed itself to that plight. Manning's commendations were mixed with criticism, especially criticism of some of the methods that Booth used to accomplish his goals. However, as early as 1882 in *The Contemporary Review*, Cardinal Manning wrote: "What, then, is the spiritual desolation of London? Let any man stand on the high northern ridge which commands London from West to East and ask himself: How many in this teeming, seething whirlpool of men have never been baptized? Have never been taught the Christian faith? Never set foot in a church? How many are living ignorantly in sin? How many with full knowledge are breaking the laws of God? What multitudes are blinded, or besotted, or maddened by drink? What sins of every kind and dye, and beyond all count, are committed day and night? It would surely be within the truth to say that half the population of London are practically without Christ and without God in the world. If this be so, then at once we can see how and why The Salvation Army exists" (Manning, "The Salvation Army," p. 7). See also Francis Power Cobb, "The Last Revival," *The Contemporary Review* 41 (August 1882), p.183.
For further information on Booth's Darkest England Scheme see the following: William Booth, " 'Darkest England,' and Other Affairs," *The War Cry*

16 (January 1891). p. 9; and Dean Farrar, "Social Amelioration," *The War Cry* 56 (May 1911). p. 2. Booth's *In Darkest England and the Way Out* was the result of many years of work of William Booth and The Salvation Army in London and throughout England. Booth's program, which he constantly referred to as "the Scheme," was an attempt to establish a complete Christian social plan for England that would be used as a model for the rest of the world. This book and its program were avidly defended by some and severely criticized by others. For criticisms, both positive and negative, which were written by Booth's contemporaries see "An American Review of Darkest England," *Review of Reviews* 4 (1891), p. 390; Thomas H. Huxley, *Evolution and Ethics* 9 vols. (New York: D. Appleton and Company, 1884); "In Darkest England: Progress Along the Way Out," *Review of Reviews* 3 (January-June 1891), p. 160-161; C. S. Loch, Bernard Bosanquet, and Philip Dwyer, *Criticisms on "General" Booth's Social Scheme* (London: Swan Sonnenschein and Son, 1891); Francis Peek, "In Darkest England and The Way Out," *The Contemporary Review* 58 (December 1890), p. 796-807; W. T. Stead, "In Darkest England and The Way Out," *Review of Reviews* 2 (July-December 1890), pp. 492-507; W. T. Stead, "The Book of the Year—In Darkest England," *Review of Reviews* 2 (July-December 1890), pp. 651-656; W. T. Stead, "The Darkest England Scheme," *Review of Reviews* 3 (January-June 1891), pp. 14-17. For a more contemporary criticism see Herman Ausubel, "General Booth's Scheme of Social Salvation," *American Historical Review* 56 (April 1951), pp. 519-525. For two contemporary works that deal at length with various aspects of Booth's Scheme see Inglis, *Churches and the Working Classes in Victorian England,* and Norris Magnuson, *Salvation in the Slums: Evangelical Social Work, 1865-1920,* The American Theological Library Association Monograph Series, No. 10 (Metuchen, New Jersey: The Scarecrow Press, 1977). Also see McKinley, *Marching to Glory,* p. 56; Needham, "Redemption and Social Reformation: A Theological Study of William Booth and His Movement," p. 165; and Green "Theological Roots of *In Darkest England and the Way Out"* in *Wesleyan Theological Journal* 25:1 (1990: 83-105).

34. The "submerged tenth" was Booth's descriptive term for the unfortunate of England's society of 1890. For example, the majority of people living in the East End of London in 1890 belonged to this category, and they constituted many of the criminals, drunkards, prostitutes, thieves, orphans, and severely impoverished who overwhelmed London at this time.

35. William Booth, *In Darkest England and the Way Out,* p. 282.

36. Ibid., p. 20.

37. Ibid., p. 179.

38. Ibid., p. 271.

39. Ibid., p. 270.

40. Ibid., p. 277.

41. Ibid., p. 267. In a similar vein, Booth stated that "I have nothing to say against those who are endeavouring to open up a way of escape without any consciousness of God's help. For them I feel only sympathy and compassion. In so far as they are endeavouring to give bread to the hungry, clothing to the naked, and above all, work to the workless, they are to that extent endeavouring to do the will of our Father which is in Heaven, and woe be unto all those who say them nay! But to be orphaned of all sense of the Fatherhood of God is surely not a secret source of strength. It is in most cases—it would be in my own—the secret of paralysis. If I did not feel my Father's hand in the darkness, and hear His voice in the silence of the night watches bidding me put my hand to this thing, I would shrink back dismayed;—but as it is I dare not" (Ibid., p.35).

42. In a lecture to cadets (those in training for Salvation Army officership) on January 24, 1924, Brigadier Fred Cox, formerly the personal secretary to William Booth, summarized this position in this way: "He believed in keeping religion first. People used to say to him in the early days, 'You know, General, we can do with your social operations, but we can't do with your religion; we don't want it.' The General would say- 'If you want my Social Work, you have got to have my Religion; they are joined together like the Siamese twins; to divide them is to slay them!' " (Fred Cox, "The Founder," Special Lecture to Cadets by Brigadier Fred Cox, General Booth's Personal Secretary, on January 4, 1924, p. 9).

43. William Booth, *In Darkest England and The Way Out*, p. 257.

44. Ibid., See also pp. 35, 205, 264, 268.

45. Ibid., p. 45. See also pp. 104, 110, 218.

46. William Booth, *To My Officers: A Letter from The General on His Eightieth Birthday*, p. 44. See also pp. 19-20; Begbie, *The Life of General William Booth*, 2: 113, 329, 331; Needham, "Redemption and Social Reformation: A Theological Study of William Booth and His Movement," pp. 74-76, 80,83-84.

CONCLUSION

AN INVITATION TO GREATER UNDERSTANDING

1. McKinley, *Marching to Glory*, p. 39.
2. Chadwick, *The Victorian Church*, 2:271.
3. Inglis, *Churches and the Working Classes in Victorian England*, p. 259.
4. Ibid., p. 197.

CREST BOOKS

Salvation Army National Publications

Crest books, a division of The Salvation Army's National Publications department, was established in 1997 so contemporary Salvationist voices could be captured and bound in enduring form for future generations, to serve as witnesses to the continuing force and mission of the Army.

Stephen Banfield and Donna Leedom, *Say Something*

Judith L. Brown and Christine Poff, eds., *No Longer Missing: Compelling True Stories from The Salvation Army's Missing Persons Ministry*

Terry Camsey, *Slightly Off Center! Growth Principles to Thaw Frozen Paradigms*

Marlene Chase, *Pictures from the Word; Beside Still Waters: Great Prayers of the Bible for Today; Our God Comes: And Will Not Be Silent*

John Cheydleur and Ed Forster, eds., *Every Sober Day Is a Miracle*

Helen Clifton, *From Her Heart: Selections from the Preaching and Teaching of Helen Clifton*

Shaw Clifton, *Never the Same Again: Encouragement for New and Not-So-New Christians; Who Are These Salvationists? An Analysis for the 21st Century; Selected Writings, Vol. 1: 1974-1999 and Vol. 2: 2000-2010*

Christmas Through the Years: A War Cry Treasury

Stephen Court and Joe Noland, eds., *Tsunami of the Spirit*

Frank Duracher, *Smoky Mountain High*

Easter Through the Years: A War Cry Treasury

Ken Elliott, *The Girl Who Invaded America: The Odyssey Of Eliza Shirley*

Ed Forster, *101 Everyday Sayings From the Bible*

William W. Francis, *Celebrate the Feasts of the Lord: The Christian Heritage of the Sacred Jewish Festivals; The Stones Cry Out; Building Blocks of Spiritual Leadership*

Henry Gariepy, *Israel L. Gaither: Man with a Mission; A Salvationist Treasury: 365 Devotional Meditations from the Classics to the Contemporary; Andy Miller: A Legend and a Legacy*

Henry Gariepy and Stephen Court, *Hallmarks of The Salvation Army*

Roger J. Green, *The Life & Ministry of William Booth* (with Abingdon Press, Nashville)

How I Met The Salvation Army

Carroll Ferguson Hunt, *If Two Shall Agree* (with Beacon Hill Press, Kansas City)

John C. Izzard, *Pen of Flame: The Life and Poetry of Catherine Baird*

David Laeger, *Shadow and Substance: The Tabernacle of the Human Heart*

John Larsson, *Inside a High Council; Saying Yes to Life*

Living Portraits Speaking Still: A Collection of Bible Studies

Herbert Luhn, *Holy Living: The Mindset of Jesus*

Paul A. Marshall, *Vignettes of Victory: Heroes, Heroines, Highlights, & Sidelights*

Philip Needham, *He Who Laughed First: Delighting in a Holy God,* (with Beacon Hill Press, Kansas City); *When God Becomes Small*

R.G. Moyles, *I Knew William Booth; Come Join Our Army; William*

Booth in America: Six Visits 1886 - 1907; Farewell to the Founder

Joe Noland, *A Little Greatness*

Quotes of the Past & Present

Lyell M. Rader, *Romance & Dynamite: Essays on Science & the Nature of Faith*

Amy Reardon, *Holiness Revealed: A Devotional Study in Hebrews* (with Wesleyan Publishing House, Indianapolis)

R. David Rightmire, *Sanctified Sanity: The Life and Teaching of Samuel Logan Brengle; The Sacramental Journal of the Salvation Army: A Study of Holiness Foundations*

Allen Satterlee, *Turning Points: How The Salvation Army Found a Different Path; Determined to Conquer: The History of The Salvation Army Caribbean Territory; In the Balance: Christ Weighs the Hearts of 7 Churches*

Harry Williams, *An Army Needs An Ambulance Corps: A History of The Salvation Army's Medical Services*

A. Kenneth Wilson, *Fractured Parables: And Other Tales to Lighten the Heart and Quicken the Spirit; The First Dysfunctional Family: A Modern Guide to the Book of Genesis, It Seemed Like a Good Idea at the Time: Some of the Best and Worst Decisions in the Bible*

A Word in Season: A Collection of Short Stories

Check Yee, *Good Morning China*

Chick Yuill, *Leadership on the Axis of Change*